from Plant *to* Plate

turning
fresh, simple
food into
a delicious
habit

LIFE
HEALTH
N E T W O R K

lifeand**health**.org

Life and Health Network is a 501(c)(3) non-profit health media organization created by a group of physicians and dentists who all share an earnest desire to do more than the norm. True health shouldn't be merely about diagnosing symptoms and prescribing medication—it is far more valuable than that.

How? Simple—balanced nutrition, regular fitness, and a positive state of mind. The goal of Life and Health Network is to seek the plain, science-backed truth and to share it with you through:

Healthy recipes, cooking videos, articles, and other wellness resources all for **free** at **life**and**health**.org.

102 El Dorado Street
Auburn, CA 95603
www.lifeandhealth.org

ISBN: 978-0-9895575-0-4
Library of Congress Control Number: 2013911330

Printed in China.

Nutritional Information Disclaimer: The nutritional information for each recipe was computed using Calorie Count software. This analytical tool uses general averages for every ingredient, and may not be 100 percent accurate or completely reflective of the brands and ingredients you are using. The statistics provided are per serving and do not account for "optional" ingredients that may or may not be listed.

To you who, through the simple act of picking up this book, have taken a small but mighty step toward a healthier life.

INTRO *a note to readers*

Dear Readers,

The journey that brought me to this exciting moment and this *thrilling* book began at age nine. My brother had come home from school and was excitedly sharing that he had learned about the health benefits of vegetarianism that day. It didn't take much to convince me and I quickly renounced meat and became a vegetarian. Even as a child, I recognized the "whole" aspect of good nutrition. In church, for example, I learned about the dietary choices Daniel and his friends made (Dan. 10:3), and I remember feeling astounded by their clear minds, spiritual fortitude, and the ways God blessed their steadfast faith. I was inspired. Sure, there were times when I missed my mom's fried chicken, but that faded with time while my appreciation for and curiosity about plant-based nutrition only deepened. The future I saw in nutrition and health was too bright to look back.

I leaped ahead to said future, heart fixed on sharing everything I learned along the way, just as my brother did when I was nine. I studied nutrition at Loma Linda University, in Loma Linda, California, and ran a consulting business for weight loss and other lifestyle diseases. (It was there that I understood the plain truth of the phrase "you are what you eat.") When I became pregnant with my first children (twin boys), I pored over countless books and studies about the prenatal effects of the mother's diet, coming to the realization that good nutrition before and during pregnancy has a significant impact on the child's physical health and overall intelligence. All of this study led to a little-considered but incredibly compelling aspect of poor nutrition: the brain. The brain's frontal lobe—the area that makes moral decisions—is directly damaged by a bad diet. This struck me. Let me explain. My single greatest joy is God, and I long to always hear Him clearly. However, if the mind, body, and spirit cannot be separated as science suggests, then the way I feed myself will affect my relationship with Christ. It all became quite straightforward from there: the Bible says that our bodies are temples of the Holy Spirit (1 Cor. 6:19) and I should treat it as such.

For some, a plant-based lifestyle comes about as a result of shocking animal cruelty or environmental documentaries. For some, it's a religious and/or cultural lifestyle choice. For me, it's a combination of all of the above, along with years of study and personal practice that brings me to believe in the power of a well-balanced, plant-based lifestyle.

I eventually settled down with my family of five in the Sacramento region. Sacramento has recently been dubbed America's "Farm-To-Fork Capital" because of its warm climate and location in the center of year-round, varied agriculture. Needless to say, it's an inspiring place to live, eat, and write this book from. It's also what gave rise to this book's title "From Plant to Plate." Although Sacramento is particularly blessed with farm-fresh produce year round, any American city with a supermarket can experience the filling and even familiar flavors of plant-to-plate cooking. I urge you to give it a try (and to visit your local farmers market whenever possible.)

As a vegan dietitian, my dream has been to help people feel better, starting with the very basic tenets of good food choices. This book allows me to share my philosophy on proper nutrition with you, the reader. Your hands turning these pages constitute a dream that has literally come true.

I hope you discover something that inspires you within these pages.

With love,

Tami Bivens

Tami Bivens, R.D.

PART ONE *the knowledge*

Health, Simplified 1.1

Although the focus of this book is food, health is a complex subject in which many different practices are interconnected. The phrase, "diet and exercise," did not come about by chance. It is important to recognize that change in diet alone is not enough to sustain good health for the long term.

To this end, we'd like to introduce you to eight simple, natural remedies, or 'health laws', which have been proven to have a strong positive influence on health and longevity. Consider them your free prescription towards better health and a longer life.

AIR

Some consider breathing to be the most important of all the bodily functions because all other functions depend on it. Life is dependent upon breathing.

In a word, breath is life. But the type of air you should be breathing is also something to consider. The "healthiest" air is oxygen-rich, negatively charged air. Negatively charged air tends to concentrate near rivers, waterfalls, beaches, forests, mountains, and, interestingly enough, areas that have just been struck by lightning. Did you notice what all of these places have in common? They all seem to congregate in the outdoors; specifically, the wild and natural outdoors. In fact, it's been discovered that the number of negative ions in any of the places just mentioned is up to 10 times more than the office or living room you're sitting in right now.

But suppose you can't make your way to the top of a mountain right now. Try growing a plant in your kitchen or on your office desk. They can be used to "grow" your own fresh air. Flush the stale air out of your lungs by taking a deep sigh once in awhile. Even better, take a moment to do so outside.

WATER

Next to air, water is the element most necessary for survival. A normal adult is 60–70% water. We can go without food for almost two months, but without water only a few days. Yet most people have no idea how much water they should drink. In fact, many live in a dehydrated state.

Without water, we'd be poisoned to death by our own waste products. When the kidneys remove uric acid and urea, these must be dissolved in water. If there isn't enough water, wastes are not removed as effectively and may build up as kidney stones. Water is also vital for chemical reactions in digestion and metabolism. It carries nutrients and oxygen to the cells through the blood and helps to cool the body through perspiration. Water also lubricates our joints.

We even need water to breathe: our lungs must be moist to take in oxygen and excrete carbon dioxide. It is possible to lose a pint of liquid each day just by exhaling.

So if you don't drink sufficient water, you can impair every aspect of your physiology. Dr. Howard Flaks, a bariatric (obesity) specialist in Beverly Hills, CA, says, "By not drinking enough water, many people incur ex-

Vitamin D is frequently called the "sunshine vitamin."

cess body fat, poor muscle tone and size, decreased digestive efficiency and organ function, increased toxicity in the body, joint and muscle soreness and water retention.

The minimum for a healthy person is 8–10 eight-ounce classes per day. A good rule of thumb for your own recommended water in take is: your body weight in pounds divided in half. That number is the recommended number of ounces you should drink each day.

SUN

It's warm, it's bright—the sun is generally thought to be a pretty happy component in our everyday lives. But why do we need it? What makes it indispensable to our lives?

Two words: Vitamin D. There is a cholesterol-like compound in our blood that transforms into vitamin

D when exposed to sunlight. This vitamin D is then converted to its active form by the liver and then by the kidneys.

Vitamin D is frequently called the "sunshine vitamin." It's necessary for normal bone mineralization and growth, maintenance of muscle strength and coordination, cardiovascular health, and robust and balanced immune function. Recent reports show that populations around the world are suffering from vitamin D deficiency. In the U.S., only ⅓ of the population is getting enough vitamin D to promote optimal health and prevent potentially severe bone-fracture rates.

Physical activity has long been known to bestow such benefits as helping to maintain a healthy weight and reduce stress, not to mention tightening the muscles.

The Fact is, the very best source of vitamin D is the sun. Our bodies use the sunlight to make vitamin D, and a deficiency could mean that you are not soaking up enough rays.

Most people only need to spend a short time in the sun to boost their mood and maintain healthy vitamin D levels. Once a person makes enough vitamin D, any extra is turned into inactive substances. Incorporate just 20-30 minutes of natural, warmth-bringing, and mood-lifting sunlight into your life and see how it works to better your overall wellness.

EXERCISE

Every New Year's Day, millions of Americans flock to the gym, armed with resolutions to get back in shape. But regular exercise is much, much more than a thinner waistline and taut abdomen. Regular workouts may actually help fight off colds and flu, reduce the risk of certain cancers and chronic diseases and slow the process of aging.

Physical activity has long been known to bestow such benefits as helping to maintain a healthy weight and reduce stress, not to mention tightening muscles. Now, a growing body of research is showing that regular exercise—as simple as a brisk 30 to 45-minute walk five times a week—can boost the body's immune system, increasing the circulation of natural killer cells that fight off viruses and bacteria. And exercise has been shown to improve the body's response to the influenza vaccine, making it more effective at keeping the virus at bay.

Medical experts say inactivity poses as great a health risk as smoking, contributing to heart disease, diabetes, hypertension, cancer, depression, arthritis, and osteoporosis. The Centers for Disease Control (CDC) says 36% of U.S. adults didn't engage in any leisure-time activity in 2008.

Even lean men and women who are inactive are at higher risk of death and disease. So while reducing obesity is an important goal, the better message would be to get everyone to walk 30 minutes a day.

REST

Most, if not all, of us can feel the effects of not getting enough sleep. It hits us hard the next morning like an overindulgent meal—we feel foggy and drained, our memory doesn't work so well, and we struggle to carry out even the simplest of tasks.

A recently published study reported that if you regularly sleep less than 7 hours each night, your immune system would suffer for it, making you three times more likely to get sick. People with little sleep also tend to be more overweight and have shorter lifespans. Research has actually shown that sleeping less alters the metabolic pathways that regulate appetite, making you feel hungrier as a result. Quality sleep on a regular basis is necessary for a robust immune system.

REM, the "deep sleep" phase of the sleep cycle is where the most intense neural activity occurs. During REM sleep, blood circulation increases, oxygen levels rise, and brain tissue absorbs more amino acids. Scientists even go so far as to say that "good sleepers" are mentally sharper and at lower risk of neurological diseases like Alzheimer's.

Even though our body might appear very still when we sleep, it's actually quite active metabolically. Free radicals—substances that have been shown to be involved in many disease processes—are gobbled up at an increased rate during sleep. Reparative processes—protein production fixing the damage our bodies sustained during the day such as sun damage—are also active.

So how much sleep do we need? Studies show that optimal health is achieved when newborns sleep 16-18 hours, young children sleep 10-12 hours, older children and teens sleep 9 hours, and adults sleep 7-8 hours. This doesn't mean that our need for sleep decreases with age. In fact, senior citizens need as much sleep as teenagers.

It might have been some time since you've felt great in the morning, but waking up with a clear mind and zest to start the day is entirely possible, and entirely worth turning off the light an hour earlier than usual. Try it for a week...then try it for the rest of your life.

TEMPERANCE

Your mind may have read "temperance" and jumped to the Temperance Movement (which prohibited the consumption of alcoholic beverages in the 1800s), but temperance is much more than simply avoiding alcohol. Try to think of temperance as a state of mind wherein you seek to practice balance with your body and your passions. It's really an age-old conflict that stretches back to ancient Greece and even to the dawn of mankind.

So how do we practice moderation in our own lives? As we mentioned earlier, we need to figure out how to control our bodies and our actions. An extremely challenging place to do this is in our diets. Obesity in much of the advanced world is becoming a widespread public health issue that, if left unchecked, will become the leading cause of death. So when it comes to your food choices, think and choose temperately. Eat enough to sustain your physical needs and choose nutrient rich foods that will make your body happy.

When it seems like our lives are spinning out of control, temperance can help us regain direction. It is about balance and control, remember? In our exceedingly digitized world, most if not all of us could probably spend much of the day with our eyes glued to some kind of screen. Where's the life in that? Where's the joy? Practice your temperance with your reliance on technology and take a moment to collect your thoughts and simply breathe. Spend a little extra time with your family and friends and engage in a real conversation without the television blaring in the background.

The true key to living a temperate lifestyle lies in our minds. We need to learn to safeguard our thoughts and carefully monitor our emotions. If you're the type to give rise to anger easily, take a few deep breaths and learn the power of forgiveness. If you're prone to bragging, give way to more humble conversation. If you're the judgmental type, give compassion a try. Think of your mind as a springboard for all of your actions. If you can learn to use your mind carefully and wisely, you will have won the battle against intemperance.

TRUST

New brain scan research has shown that spiritual practices can actually improve memory and may even slow down the aging process itself. In the book How God Changes Your Brain by Dr. Andrew Newberg, extensive research and brain scans show that spiritual practices are inherently good for our bodies—especially our brains. According to Newberg, both meditation and prayer play significant roles in strengthening import-

New brain scan research has shown that spiritual practices can actually improve memory and may even slow down the aging process itself.

ant circuits in our brains, which makes us more socially aware and alert, while simultaneously reducing anxiety, depression, and neurological stress.

So consider this: Does trust in a divine power play a role in our goal to live long and healthy lives?

In a study entitled "Religious involvement and U.S. adult mortality," it was found that people who never attended religious activities exhibited close to twice the risk of death, compared with those attending religious activities more than once a week. This amounts to a seven-year difference in life expectancy. In other words, the health benefit of regularly attending religious activities is comparable to not smoking!

Ever consider the phrase "power of prayer"? Academics show that prayer has beneficial health effects, particularly for the person who is doing the praying. Studies of "petitionary prayer," or prayer in which a person prays for her own health or peace of mind, show tangible statistical results. Science backs up the benefits of praying for your own health, especially when it comes to mental health issues such as clinical depression.

So does God change our brains? Or, as our Creator, does God know that makes us the healthiest? It's highly possible. When we allow Him into our lives, our brains are "turned on," our bodies are made more efficient, our immune systems are strengthened, and our thinking becomes clearer. In our goal to live sustainable lives, being firmly rooted in God and fellowshipping with likeminded believers has been shown to be one of the most effective strategies.

My suggestion? Consider stepping into your local church this weekend. It wouldn't hurt.

NUTRITION

Over the last several decades, we've been trained to want a "faster" and "easier" mode of doing just about everything. We have timesaving gadgets and options so plentiful that the idea of cooking a simple, healthy meal rather than going through a drive-through window seems old-fashioned and impractical.

The goal for those of us trying to maintain or improve our health is to prepare most of our foods from ingredients that are healthy. Ideally, much of our food will come from our own gardens, or from our local farmers markets, or, at the very least, won't be packed full of chemicals and disease.

The next time you go to the supermarket, shop at the edges of the store because that's where a lot of the good stuff lives. Things like fruits, vegetables, nuts, and grains are often found around the perimeter. Ironically, the things in boxes often live in the center of the store. These "center-aisle' products are often highly processed and their origins, as well as their nutritional value, can be ill-defined.

In our fast-paced society, we need to develop strategies that reduce prep time. Cooking may be a social thing, but people usually just want to get it done and then move on. By eating more of our foods raw, we can obviously reduce prep time while getting the highest nutrition possible from that product.

Other strategies can be developed that make prep time about the same as going to a fast food restaurant. For example, you can cook a large meal and store the second half of it in your freezer for another day. Cooking meals ahead of time and freezing them is an excellent way to provide you with an easy meal on a busy day. Some foods, which are used in many different dishes, can be prepared at the beginning of the week and stored in the refrigerator. This will save you the step of chopping, cutting, or peeling later on.

Ultimately time, not money, seems to be the biggest reason people don't cook. People often say that they simply don't have the time to shop for food, fix it for themselves, and eat "right" in general. If you belong to this group, consider this: calculations have shown have that, for every minute of exercise, you gain two minutes in longevity. Doubtless, the same positive adjustment will be found when you choose to cook and eat healthy food instead of a hyper-processed food product tossed into the deep fat fryer by a nameless someone. The average American, regardless of income level, watches no less than 90 minutes of television per day. Take 45 of those TV-watching minutes and dedicate them to cooking yourself a simple, healthful dinner. You'll be able to do it with time to spare, we assure you! The time is there; you simply need to prioritize.

For obvious reasons, we're zooming in on this aspect of health for the rest of the cookbook.

Introduction to a Plant-Based Diet 1.2

WHY GO PLANT-BASED RIGHT NOW?

You may have noticed that, in the past decade or so, vegetarianism and particularly veganism have become somewhat "cool." Nowadays, there tend to be more plant-based options on restaurant menus than "salad" or "garden burger." 100 percent vegen restaurants like

Native Foods Café in Los Angeles, California are rapidly gaining in popularity among omnivores and vegetarians alike. People seem to be searching for something better than the meat and potatoes that was a standard on American tables since the beginning of our history.

But why is this happening now? What brought you to purchase and read this book? It may be the result of many issues coming to a head. Obesity is an epidemic, along with diabetes, heart disease, and countless other diet-related ailments. Most of us spend the majority of our days and evenings sitting—in front of our computers at work or

in front of our televisions at home. Most restaurants and even our own pantries are brimming with high-fat, high-sodium, high-cholesterol foods in enormous portions that do nothing but provide immediate gratification and permanent damage. In brief, our lifestyles have grown increasingly sick, and we know that we must do something about it.

And so now we're here—you and I— leafing through a book about change and simplicity. But vegetarianism, an even veganism, is nothing new. People have been making the change throughout history; their reasons are varied, but they boil down to a few simple categories. Let's take a look.

RELIGIOUS TRADITION.

Many world religions promote a vegetarian diet based on the belief that killing for food when other options are available is morally wrong, or based on the belief that we are spiritually responsible for our physical bodies. Now that factory farming has become widespread, disease-laden meat products and animal welfare concerns underscore the imperative to avoid consuming animal products based on both these religious principles. The first precept of Buddhism is to avoid killing any living being; thus, most Buddhists are vegetarian. Many Hindus are also vegetarian. Important aspects of Hinduism are reincarnation and karma, and Hindus believe that all souls, upon death, are reborn as another person or animal. Out of respect for these souls, many Hindus follow a vegetarian diet.

The Jain religion shares these ideas of reincarnation, karma, and nonviolence, but is perhaps unique in that vegetarianism is uncompromisingly demanded of all its followers. The Jewish religion also has ties to vegetarianism, from ancient groups such as the Essenes to modern Jews. Many base their vegetarianism on the fact that the first diet commanded by God was a vegetarian one: "God also said, 'I give you all plants that bear seed everywhere on earth, and every tree bearing fruit which yields seed: they shall be yours for food.'"

Throughout history, Christians have also practiced vegetarianism. Christianity teaches compassion and sanctity to life. However, the cruelty often found in today's factory farms can be hard to reconcile with that ethic. The Bible also obligates Christians to respect their physical bodies. For example, 1 Corinthians 6:19 declares that our bodies are "the temple of God," and Christians interpret this as a call to temperance in diet and lifestyle. Knowing the deleterious effects of animal-based foods, especially as advances in nutrition, ecology, and agriculture shed further light, Christian principles favor a plant-based diet.

NONVIOLENCE TOWARD ALL LIFE.

Nonviolence toward all forms of life is a concept that's prevailed in many traditions. In the thirteenth century, St. Francis of Assisi said, "If you have men who will exclude any of

God's creatures from the shelter of compassion and pity, you will have men who will deal likewise with their fellow men." Isn't that striking? It hits at the heart of who we are

Environmental concerns aside, the fact is clear: if the world were to give up the practice of eating meat, we would have accomplished the greatest step toward ending starvation across the entire planet.

as human beings. Can we really live peaceful, loving, and self-sacrificing lives when we're simultaneously taking the lives of animals for food? And could violence toward animals perpetuate violence toward each other?

Leo Tolstoy believed this, stating, "As long as there are slaughterhouses, there will be battlefields." These words are especially relevant today in light of dirty, sprawling, machine-like factory farms and the downright abusive conditions therein. Gone are the days of the small family farm where cows, pigs, and chickens roamed freely and grazed at leisure. Today, animals are fed unnatural fodder and are injected with drug after drug. This is done not only to prevent the disease that is likely to spread in such unsanitary conditions, but also because factory farmers have found that certain drugs accelerate tissue growth and milk production. Basically, the lives of factory farm animals are now moving at warp speed with the help of drugs. Their lives are for one purpose: to be turned into food as cost-effectively as possible.

Consider a quote by Gandhi, in which he claims "The greatness of a nation and its moral progress can be judged by the way its animals are treated." Given this statement and the current conditions of our farm animals, what's become of our morals?

SUSTAINING THE ENVIRONMENT AND, ULTIMATELY, HUMAN LIFE.

The ethics of a plant-based diet stretch far beyond the cost of animal life, especially today. We see messages about "greening" our planet everywhere: on T-shirts, billboards, even in movie plots. How does eating meat factor into this message?

Today, factory farming accounts for 37% of methane emissions. Methane has more than twenty times the global-warming potential of carbon dioxide. The use of fossil fuels on factory farms to grow feed and to intensively raise land animals for food emits ninety million tons of carbon dioxide worldwide each year. Globally, deforestation for animal grazing and feed crops is estimated to emit 2.4 billion tons of carbon dioxide every year. According to a study done by the Environmental Integrity Project, some factory farm test sites in the United States registered pollution emission levels well above Clean Air Act health-based limits.

Environmental concerns aside, the fact is clear: if the world were to give up the practice of eating meat, we would have accomplished the greatest step toward ending starvation across the entire planet. The following fact was reported by David Pimentel, professor of ecology at Cornell University: "If all the grain currently fed to livestock in the United States were consumed directly by people, the number of people who could be fed would be nearly 800 million."

The words of Albert Einstein ring true: "Nothing will benefit human health and increase chances for survival on Earth as much as the evolution to a vegetarian diet."

OUR HEALTH.

Now let's put the well-being of animal species, our planet, and hungry continents aside for a moment. Let's focus on you and your personal health.

Going as far back as ancient Babylon, there are those who have understood the benefits of a plant-based diet. Take, for example, the biblical story of Daniel and his friends found in Daniel chapter 1. The chapter records what is perhaps the first "study" on plant-based nutrition ever recorded. Daniel and his friends, who desired to follow a vegetarian diet, were tested against the rest of their classmates who ate "the king's meat." The result? Daniel and

shown that a clearer mind, improved mental capacity and performance, and heightened awareness of spiritual issues are often results of maintaining a plant-based lifestyle. Benjamin Franklin, who was often chided for

"Let thy food be thy medicine."

his friends were found by the king to be ten times healthier and wiser than all of their classmates.

In addition to this, many of the ancient Greeks and Romans acknowledged and studied the incredible value of a healthful diet. Hippocrates, often considered to be the founder of Western medicine, famously admonished mankind to, "Let thy food be thy medicine." Many of the ancient philosophers themselves were vegetarians (or at least ate very little meat). In fact, until just a couple hundred years ago, the vegetarian diet was actually referred to as the "Pythagorean diet" in honor of Pythagoras, a Greek philosopher, mathematician (remember the Pythagorean theorem?), and vegetarian advocate.

It's not only your physical health—your brain likes plants too. It's been

his vegetarian diet, said that he was rewarded with "Greater clearness of head and quicker comprehension."

It's pretty incredible when you consider the context of then and now. Back then, meat production looked very different from the large-scale, machine-like production it is today. Simply put, it was much more natural and wholesome because natural and wholesome was all they could afford. Ironic, isn't it? Now, we should pay special heed to their advice, as the quality of animal products today is nothing short of troublesome.

YOU SEE, IT'S ALL INTERCONNECTED.

As you navigate your way through this book, keep all of the above "reasons" in mind. Speaking from my own personal experience and the testimonies of many friends and family members, it's simply unsustainable to just pick one reason off the list and embark on a vegan journey with full confidence. Often, those who choose a vegan lifestyle simply for the sake of their religion, simply for the environment, etc., are found to be nutritionally deficient. The aspects of *nutrition* and *health* cannot be left unexamined, in the same way that the ethical factors shouldn't be ignored.

Do you know the old Indian proverb, "Everyone is a house with four rooms: a physical, a mental, an emotional, and a spiritual"? The proverb says that every day, we need to spend a bit of time in each room, even if only to give it a breath of fresh air. This concept is paralleled in the Gospel of Luke. In it, Luke writes that Jesus "Increased in *wisdom* and *stature,* and in favor with *God* and *man.*"

LIVE LIKE A SEVENTH-DAY ADVENTIST

An article published by *U.S. News & World Report* gave several tips for those looking to live to one hundred. One of those tips was: "Live

like a Seventh-day Adventist". Many studies have shown that Adventists live longer, healthier lives. In fact, American Seventh-day Adventists are known to have an average life expectancy of eighty-nine years—around a decade longer than the average American. A major factor in this is the focus that the Adventist Church has placed on health.

Based on their beliefs about honoring God with their bodies (1 Cor. 6:19-20), many Adventists follow vegetarian or vegan diets. However, physical health is not the only goal of these diets. Seventh-day Adventists understand health in a holistic way; they believe that physical, mental, and spiritual health cannot be divorced from one another. In addition to diet, Adventists also emphasize the importance of exercise, abstinence from alcohol and drugs, and observing the Sabbath (a day of rest).

The health and longevity of Seventh-day Adventists are so intriguing that they've been made the subjects of hundreds of articles in multiple medical journals. The most recent of these appeared in the *Journal of the American Medical Association* (JAMA). Released in June 2013, the study tracked the health of over 70,000 Seventh-day Adventist Christians. It found, yet again, that

The health and longevity of Seventh-day Adventists are so intriguing that they've been made the subjects of hundreds of articles in multiple medical journals.

a lower risk of death was associated with the vegetarian diets that Adventists tend to follow.

So if you're someone who tends to walk through life seeing only a very tiny sliver of the world around you, how would that change if you considered the greater consequences of our actions and choices? A plant-based diet is about being as compassionate, as conscientious, and as healthy as possible. It is so much more than a diet. It's a lifestyle—we think it's a good one—and its benefits are far-reaching.

Welcome to your journey!

Making Sense Of The Labels 1.3

As your food lifestyle evolves to a simpler, whole foods, and plant-based lifestyle, you may start paying closer attention to food labels. Grocery shopping turns into an *experience*, as you search and read and examine labels to discover which tomato or brand of oats is the most nutritious.

In the beginning, I wondered, Is this a waste of time or even necessary? Then, I began to see it as an extremely worthy treasure hunt for my family and I. It may take more time to shop this way, but it goes to lengths to ensure that I know what's going into my body, and helps me to better understand my own food choices. It's therapeutic, really, as I've settled into a little rhythm at the farmers market or grocery store, syncopated only by the occasional new seasonal fruit or vegetable.

That's not to say this lifestyle might not be daunting at first. Deciphering nutrition labels can at first be like reading hieroglyphics. A 2011 study published in the *Journal of the American Dietetic Association* showed that less than 10% of participants looked at the calorie content of a nutrition label. Understandably so. There are so many confusing terms; who can be expected to keep up?

Well, maybe we can try. Let's put ourselves to the challenge, shall we? Starting with the following:

"HIGH"

In order for a food label to claim that their product is high in a nutrient (e.g., high in fiber), one must provide 20% of the Daily Value. If the food contains 10-19%, then it's considered a "good" source.

"LOW CARB"

Surprisingly, there are no set guidelines for this claim. (What's going on, Food and Drug Administration?) This leaves a lot of room for misleading labels and frivolous purchasing. Often, when a high carbohydrate food is modified to become a low-carbohydrate food, the fat and calorie content go up. It's better to choose foods that are naturally low in carbohydrates, such as nuts (in moderation), tofu, and of course, vegetables.

"LOW SODIUM"

Foods that claim to be low sodium must contain 140 milligrams or less per serving. The 2010 Dietary Guidelines for Americans recommend less than 2,300 milligrams per day to prevent hypertension and risk for stroke. Pay close attention to this label. As a general rule, if there is 1mg of sodium (or less) for every 1 calorie, you can consider the food within a safe sodium level.

"BPA-FREE"

BPA stands for bisphenol A, which is an industrial chemical used to make certain plastics, particularly those used in the food industry. The American Chemistry Council stands by their claim that products that contain BPA pose no risk to consumers, but other associations feel different-

ly. There are various products that are BPA-free including cans, baby products, and beverage containers.

"NON-GMO"

Genetically-modified organisms (GMOs) are crops that have been modified in a lab to remain resistant to herbicides or increase nutritional content. Often referred to as "Frankenfood," this experimental practice represents 80% of North American crops, yet 53% of consumers claim they wouldn't buy something that's been genetically modified. To be absolutely certain about the status of your favorite food, check out the **Non-GMO Project**, which provides a complete list of foods that have gone through their rigorous verification process. Large food companies are also taking the guesswork out of GMOs.

"ENRICHED"

Not to be confused with "fortified," enriched means that some of the nutrients have been added back into a food that may have lost them during the refining process. People often think that this means the food has *additional* vitamins and minerals, but that's not the case. Food companies simply put back what was once there. The most common example of this is enriched flour. During the refining process, many essential nutrients are lost, and during the enriching process, some are put back in.

"FORTIFIED"

The fortification means that an item has added vitamins and minerals in addition to the ones that are naturally occurring. Plenty of foods are fortified to ensure adequate nutrition for the general population.

CALORIES

A calorie is the currency unit for energy provided by food. There is a calorie requirement for the human body to run and function properly, and this value varies for each individual depending on a number of different factors such as metabolic rate and physical activity. When this calorie requirement is exceeded, the body will store fat, thus resulting in weight gain. When the calorie requirement is not met, the body will draw needed energy from fat stores, thus resulting in weight loss.

The Harris-Benedict equation is a good formula for calculating calories needed per day. BMR=655+(4.35 x weight in pounds)+(4.7 x height in inches)-(4.7 x age in years). You just need to plug in your weight, height and years. The number you get is the total number of calories you need to exist per day. A 50 yr old woman who weighs 160 lbs and is 5' 7" will have a basil metabolic rate (BMR) of 1440 calories per day. If you do more than lay around all day, you will need more calories. In the end, counting calories is important but eating a balanced, healthy diet and getting at least 30 minutes of vigorous exercise per day is the key to keeping your caloric intake in balance.

FAT

Fat is essential for a body to function properly, and it is recommended that 20-35% of one's calorie intake come from fats and oils, about 45 grams of fat per day. However, not all fats are created equal. Polyunsaturated and monounsaturated fats are the "healthy fats" that lower your blood cholesterol and protect your heart. These mainly come from plant sources such as avocados and nuts.

Saturated and trans fats are the "bad fats" that elevate blood cholesterol and increase your risk of heart disease. They mainly come from animal sources such meat and dairy products and partially hydrogenated vegetable oils. It is recommended that one consume less than 10% of calories from saturated fat and avoid all trans fats

90% of Americans over the age of two consume too much sodium in their diet.

in one's diet. While different fats serve to either benefit or harm the body, they contain the same number of calories per gram and are calorie dense. Therefore, one should pay attention to the overall calories they consume from fats in order to maintain a healthy weight.

CHOLESTEROL

Cholesterol is a necessary element in building structure and fluidity in the body's cell membranes. However, dietary cholesterol is unnecessary for consumption since the body already produces the amount of cholesterol needed to function properly. Dietary cholesterol is found only in animal sources and can increase one's risk for developing high blood cholesterol and plaque buildup in arteries, which will eventually lead to heart disease and stroke. Limit cholesterol intake to as little possible. Remember, all plant-based recipes are cholesterol free!

SODIUM

90% of Americans over the age of two consume too much sodium in their diet. The main dietary sources of sodium are processed foods and typical restaurant fare. Therefore, by eating a whole foods, plant-based diet, one can greatly decrease the amount of sodium in one's diet. A high-sodium diet can lead to high blood pressure and increase the risk of heart disease, kidney disease, and stroke. It is recommended to limit sodium to less than 2,300 milligrams (two teaspoons) of salt per day.

CARBOHYDRATES

The total number of carbohydrates includes added sugar, complex carbohydrates, and fiber. Carbohydrates are the ideal source of energy for our bodies to use instead of protein and fat, because they can most easily be converted to glucose, the form of sugar that is transported and utilized by the body. There are simple carbohydrates and complex carbohydrates. Complex carbohydrates include starch and dietary fiber that slows down the uptake of sugar and thus sustains the body longer. Simple carbohydrates are naturally found in fruits and vegetables, but also found in refined foods such as white bread, sweets, and soda. Eating refined and processed carbohydrates stripped of dietary fiber can cause health risks such as type 2 diabetes. It is recommended that one consume 45-65% of one's calories from carbohydrates.

DIETARY FIBER

Fiber is a form of carbohydrates that cannot be digested, but still provides necessary benefits for a healthy body. Dietary fiber comes in two forms: soluble and insoluble fiber. Soluble fiber attracts water and forms a gel, which slows down the digestive process and makes you feel fuller longer. Insoluble fiber does not dissolve in water, and acts as a laxative, helping to prevent constipation. Fiber is especially important in regulating the rate at which sugar that is consumed is absorbed into the bloodstream. Foods that are processed and refined have little-to-no fiber, while fresh, whole foods contain loads of fiber. For women, it is recommended to consume 25 grams of fiber a day, and for men, 38 grams of fiber a day. As a rule, try to eat at least 14 grams of fiber for every 1,000 calories.

SUGAR

The amount of sugar represents the grams of added sugars from sweeteners such as sugar, corn syrup and honey. By looking at the ingredient list of a food product or recipe, you can determine the sources of the sugar content. As a general guide, the bigger the difference between "total carbohydrates" and "sugar," the more nutritious carbohydrates in the food. The amount of added sugar should be as low as possible, because added sugars contain no fiber, which can cause spikes in blood sugar, and can lead to insulin insensitivity and type 2 diabetes.

PROTEIN

Protein is a part of every cell, tissue, and organ in our body, and is constantly being broken down and replaced due to cell growth and degradation. Protein is broken down into amino acids, which are the building blocks for the protein needed by the body. Our bodies synthesize all the amino acids except nine, which

While many believe that sufficient protein cannot be provided by adopting a vegetarian or vegan diet, this is a common myth.

must come from our diet and thus are termed "the nine essential amino acids." Complete protein sources contain all essential amino acids and come from animal sources such as meat, eggs, and diary products. Incomplete protein sources don't contain all essential amino acids, but when eaten in complementary pairs with other incomplete protein sources, will provide all of the essential amino acids. While many believe that sufficient protein cannot be provided by a vegetarian or vegan diet, this is a common myth. It is recommended that 10-35% of one's daily intake of calories come from protein. Humans need 45-55 grams of protein per day.

"But, What About Your Protein Intake?" 1.4

Yes, this absolutely deserves a section of its own.

Usually, the plant-based journey begins with that question. You'll hear it often. Maybe every time it comes up that you're a vegan, or at least trying to be. The question is so common that there are buttons and T-shirts for sale that say, "Please don't ask me about my protein." There's even a silly cartoon out on the web that says, "Nobody cared about my protein intake until I became a vegan."

OK, so maybe all of that is a little dramatic, but it helps to know why you do what you do (hence this sec-

tion of the book, "The Knowledge"). The staff at Life and Health have told you much of what we know about overall health, cooking ingredients, and all kinds of cooking gadgetry, but this little protein chart might prove the most useful to you in your daily interactions with friends and family.

The point of the following chart is pretty self-explanatory: you can get plenty—and we mean *plenty*—of protein without meat, eggs, and dairy. See for yourself:

PROTEIN	g/serving
Tempeh (4 ounces)	41
Seitan (3 ounces)	31
Lentils (1 cup cooked)	18
Cannellini beans (1 cup cooked)	17
Black beans (1 cup cooked)	15
Chickpeas (1 cup cooked)	15
Kidney beans (1 cup cooked)	15
Great Northern beans (1 cup cooked)	15
Pinto beans (1 cup cooked)	14
Edamame (½ cup cooked)	11
Chia seeds (4 tablespoons)	12
Tofu (4 ounces)	10
Green peas (1 cup cooked)	9
Millet (1 cup cooked)	8.4
Quinoa (1 cup cooked)	8
Peanut butter (2 tablespoons)	8
Soy milk (1 cup)	8
Sunflower seeds (4 tablespoons)	8
Almonds (¼ cup)	7
Oat bran (1 cup cooked)	7
Whole-wheat bread (2 slices)	7
Brown rice (1 cup cooked)	5
Corn (1 large cob)	5
Spinach (1 cup cooked)	5
Broccoli (1 cup cooked)	4

There might be a few people who take a look at this chart and tell you that you're still just eating incomplete proteins. My advice? Don't worry about it. The problem with the complete/incomplete protein concern is this: *it assumes we only eat one type of food!*

It's an example of a common mistake in the nutrition field: focusing on the specific nutrients of one food without seeing it in the context of an entire diet. Saying a protein is incomplete ignores the bigger picture and is often used as a critique of vegetarianism.

While it's tempting to want to combine these "incomplete" proteins to form a whole, the truth is there is no need to combine protein sources within a given meal. Our bodies pool the amino acids we need as we eat them, and we use them when needed.

You'll be just fine, as long as you eat a variety of the above protein-containing foods on a daily basis. If you think about it, that in itself is a reflection this book has been saying all along: eat **fresh** foods, **simply**, and in a **balanced** manner.

Making Plant-Based Substitutions 1.5

When moving to a plant-based diet, cooking without foods such as butter, eggs, or cream can seem daunting. However, there are substitutions available and you'll be surprised at how well they work. Some of these substitutions have been around for ages, perhaps arising from necessity during economic hardship, while other methods were inspired by cooking techniques from other cultures. Although some may seem counterintuitive, give them a try; you'll be glad you did.

Just follow this basic formula:
When a recipe calls for _____ , use _____ instead.

For example, when a recipe calls for meat, choose any one of the following substitutions, like **Ground Bulgur "Meat"** (p. 204), or tofu, or mushrooms, etc.

MEAT

Ground Bulgur "Meat" (p. 204)

Tofu

Mushrooms

Seitan (wheat gluten)

Eggplant

Beans

Tempeh

MEAT BROTH

Vegetable broth

Vegetable bouillon cubes, prepared as directed

BUTTER

Non-hydrogenated margarine, like Earth Balance

Coconut oil

⅓ cup vegetable oil = one stick of butter

BUTTERMILK

Soy milk with acid: Mix 1 cup soy milk with 1 teaspoon apple cider vinegar or lemon juice. Then, let the mixture sit until it separates.

CONDENSED MILK

Canned coconut milk (note: coconut milk does not give food a coconut flavor, just a creamy taste, color and texture)

EGGS

1 tablespoon ground flaxseed and 3 tablespoons water = 1 egg (combine and let sit for a few minutes before using)

¼ cup applesauce = 1 egg

1 overripe mashed banana = 1 egg

HEAVY CREAM

Canned coconut milk: Put a can of coconut milk in the fridge for 48 hours. Open, and use just the solidified top layer.

MILK

Soy milk

Almond milk

Rice milk

Oat milk

Coconut milk

Hemp milk

CHEESE

Crumbled tofu in place of cottage cheese or ricotta cheese (see **Tofu-Basil Lasagna** p. 116)

Nacho Cheese-Style Sauce (p. 270)

Cashew Cheese Sauce (p. 273)

Nutritional yeast flakes

MAYONNAISE

Vegan mayonnaise: Available in canola oil, expeller-pressed canola oil, grape seed oil, and organic expeller-pressed soybean varieties

HONEY*

Agave nectar

Molasses

Maple syrup

Brown rice syrup

Date syrup

*Because honey is produced by bees, it is not plant-based. However, honey is loaded with heart healthy antioxidants and is healthier than refined sugars. If it's easier for you, use honey in the recipes instead of other listed sweeteners.

PART TWO *the prep work*

Rather than living in the midst of edible temptation, begin with the basics for a plant-based lifestyle. Below, you'll find suggested staples for your refrigerator, pantry, and freezer.

My tip? Stop by your parents' or grandparents' house and give their pantry a once-over. Their generation had far fewer processed foods. In fact, whether by necessity or choice, meat wasn't as cheap (and of such poor quality) a few decades ago as it is now.

NOTE: Before lengthy grocery store receipts start dancing before your eyes, please remember that you don't have to buy everything right away! It may be less overwhelming to pick up a few items listed in each section every time you go to the grocery store. For example, try adding a different kind of fruit to your cart, then using this cookbook's index for tasty ways to prepare it. Most of the items listed can be found at grocery stores nationwide. Purchase them bit by bit (or, of course, many at once), and you'll

soon be well stocked with a varied vegan kitchen...and ready to test out some recipes.

REFRIGERATOR

Fruits

You could flavor candy to taste like apples, lemons or berries, but why not go straight to the source? From staples like apples to more rare treats like passion fruits, fruit adds natural sweetness to your meal plan—not waistline guilt. Just like you enjoy the variety of colors in a rainbow, aim for a range of different kinds of fruits.

• Apples

• Oranges

• Bananas—Store bananas outside the fridge until ripe, then eat or freeze immediately. To ripen bananas more quickly store them in a paper bag with an apple. Because of the ethylene gas that bananas produce, they can also be used to ripen other foods, such as avocados, more quickly, with this method.

• Kiwis

• Lemons

• Berries (blackberries, raspberries, strawberries)

Vegetables

With so many different ones to choose among, filling your plate with vegetables can be a delicious adventure. Choose a variety of colors and flavors, and particularly ones with vibrant hues—they generally have the most nutrients.

• Kale

• Cabbage (green, red, Savoy, bok choy, Napa, brussels sprouts)

• Spinach

• Dark salad greens

• Bell peppers (red, yellow, orange)

• Asparagus

• Scallions

• Sprouts, assorted

• Mushrooms (cremini, Portobello, shiitake, white)

• Broccoli

• Cauliflower

• Carrots

• Tomatoes (technically not a vegetable, but usually prepared as one)

• Avocados (technically not a vegetable, but usually prepared as one)

Fresh Herbs

Brighten a dish instantly with any of the following. Generally stirred or added during the final stages of a recipe, keep herbs fresh by putting them in a container of water in the refrigerator, wrapped with a paper towel to absorb moisture, and covered with a plastic bag.

• Basil

• Cilantro

• Flat-leaf parsley

• Rosemary

• Thyme

Odds & Ends

This section is not your grandmother's scrap bag. Wake up to jam that smacks of the fruit it came from, scraped across piping hot toast. Or, use flaxseed to thicken the texture of your favorite baked goods, and make you healthier for it (flaxseed contain Omega-3s in abundance).

- Soy, nut, and seed milks (rice, almond, soy, coconut)

- Flaxseed, raw and/or ground (or buy whole seeds and grind them fresh)

- Tofu and/or tempeh

- Vegan buttery spread (with non-hydrogenated oil)

- All-fruit jam

- Hummus

- Salad vinaigrettes

FREEZER

Capture the health of fruit, vegetable, and whole-grain basics in cold storage. Whether you need to pull together a quick meal after a long day at work, or want to store leftovers for the long term, the convenience of a freezer is difficult to beat.

- Frozen brown rice

- Frozen peas, corn, and various vegetable medleys

- Frozen bananas (for green smoothies and **One-Ingredient Banana Ice Cream** p. 228)

- Frozen berries

- Whole-grain bread

PANTRY

I know the storage room (or cupboard) as a pantry, and your grandmother might have called it a larder or storehouse. Large, small, or somewhere in between, we suggest a few items that keep best at room temperature—ready for you to cook with until they're "just right."

Vegetables

Before they belong in your mouth, some vegetables should be kept out of the refrigerator for best taste. If your house is relatively warm, consider parking the following items in the garage, or another cool, dark place, which helps to keep them fresh. As with many other produce items, discard if they develop too many soft spots. For potatoes and sweet potatoes, discard immediately if you notice any color changes, which can indicate developing toxicity.

- Onions (red and/or yellow)

- Garlic

- Sweet potatoes

- Russet potatoes

- Winter squash (seasonal)

Beans & Legumes

Beans and legumes are one of the best ways to make the most of a vegetarian diet. Savor the process (quicker than you might think) of turning dried beans into a delicious dish.

- Lentils (black, brown, red, green)
- Beans (pinto, black Mayocoba, Great White Northern, etc.)
- Chickpeas (also known as garbanzo beans)
- Split peas

Sauces & Seasonings

Liven up an ordinary meal with the short list of ingredients below or blend to create sauces and dressings.

- Organic extra-virgin olive oil
- Extra-virgin coconut oil
- Extra-virgin olive oil cooking spray
- Raw agave nectar
- Pure maple syrup
- Bragg Liquid Aminos—This soy sauce substitute is better because it is non-fermented, non-GMO, and gluten free (many soy sauces have wheat). As a bonus, it contains 16 essential amino acids which will help you build a complete protein profile in your non-meat diet. Bragg is easy to find in any grocery store but if you want, just substitute soy sauce in the recipes when it calls for Bragg.
- Low-sodium soy sauce

Canned Goods

With a twist of a can opener, ingredients for your quick and healthy meal or cooking project are at the ready. Look for cans labeled BPA free or similarly to avoid potentially toxic BPA, bisphenol A, often used in certain plastics and resins.

- Lower-sodium tomato/marinara sauce
- Low-sodium vegetable broth or bouillon
- Canned tomatoes, no salt added
- Light coconut milk
- Canned beans

Grains

When you're cooking to feed a healthy habit, a (whole) grainy dish is exactly what you're aiming for. Enjoy discovering less common grains, such as quinoa or millet, or stick to familiar favorites like brown rice. When shopping for crackers, bread, etc., seek out items that say "100%

whole grain" to avoid products that sneak in white flour that's been stripped of its natural nutrients. For a nutty, rich taste, and extra nutritional benefits, look for "sprouted grains" on the ingredients list.

- Barley
- Couscous
- Rolled old-fashioned oats
- Brown rice
- Millet
- Quinoa
- Wild rice
- Whole-grain flours (wheat, light spelt, oat, almond meal, kamut, brown rice)
- Whole-grain pastas (wheat, rice, quinoa, spelt, kamut, millet)
- Whole-grain bread (whole wheat and/or gluten free)
- Tortillas (stone-ground corn or other whole grain)

Nuts, Seeds & Dried Fruit

Nuts and seeds provide satisfaction in the form of protein, fiber, healthy fats, and great taste. Toasted, they also add crunch to baked goods. When you're craving something sweet (and want to stay on the health-conscious straight and narrow), dried fruit are the best choice for quick energy. Of course, you could also make the best of both these worlds with an easy homemade trail mix or granola.

- Raw almonds
- Raw cashews
- Raw walnuts
- Sunflower seeds
- Chia seeds
- Whole flaxseed
- Sesame seeds
- Pumpkin seeds
- Raisins
- Cranberries
- Medjool dates

Sweeteners

Thanks to Mary Poppins, we all know that a spoonful of sugar makes the medicine go down. No meal plan is complete without a little bit of sweetness, so try cooking with one of the sweeteners below. Each has their own unique flavor, so enjoy trying different kinds in your quest for sweet satisfaction. As with all sweets, take care to enjoy them sparingly.

- Raw agave nectar
- Molasses
- Pure maple syrup
- Dark brown sugar
- Sucanat

Odds & Ends

Here we suggest the odds and ends that make cooking and everyday eating a little more special.

- Nut and seed butters (sunflower butter, raw almond butter, tahini, roasted natural peanut butter)
- Unsweetened applesauce
- Shelf-stable unsweetened non-dairy milks (e.g. soy, almond, rice milks)

Spices & Baking

Whether you're preparing an elaborate dish or simply a quick and healthy dinner, we suggest the following for a starter seasoning and baking kit.

- Aluminum-free baking powder
- McKay's Chicken Style Instant Broth and Seasoning
- McKay's Beef Style Instant Broth and Seasoning
- Baking soda

- Ground cinnamon
- Sea salt
- Basil
- Garlic powder
- Paprika (smoked)
- Oregano
- Ground cumin
- Cayenne pepper
- Chili powder
- Ginger
- Turmeric
- Curry powder
- Pure vanilla extract
- Raw cacao powder and/or unsweetened cocoa
- Nutritional yeast flakes—a great way to give a pungent, nutty and cheesy flavor to foods. Nutritional yeast is an inactive yeast made from sugar cane and beet molasses. It comes in flake or powder form and is different from active yeasts used in bread making. Nutritional yeast flakes is high in B vitamins, including B12, and can be found in the bulk section of health food stores, some regular grocery stores and online. Be sure not to confuse it with brewer's yeast which is an active yeast and has a bitter flavor.

TOOLS THAT YOU MUST HAVE (TO MAKE LIFE A LOT EASIER)

Cookbooks

As you become acquainted with both your kitchen and this book, you may fall in love with the cookbook-to-plate process. There's really nothing like thumbing through the sturdy pages of a cookbook, discovering an intriguing recipe, gathering all of the ingredients together, preparing it (maybe even tweaking it a bit to suit your needs), and then sitting down to enjoy the result.

High-speed blender

There are a plethora of blenders out there, ranging from $15 to $500, and most of them work perfectly fine. However, did you know that a good high-speed blender can be used to make soups, sauces, and ice creams? I'd like to introduce you to the high-speed blender, with models such as VitaMix or BlendTec.

In my opinion, the high-speed blender's greatest asset is the massively reduced time it takes to prep your ingredients. For example, rather than dicing a carrot for a carrot puree, you can simply put the entire carrot (or carrots) into a blender and let it do all the work. No stopping, stirring, or working in batches. I'm beginning to sound like an infomercial at this point, but my VitaMix is *such* a tremendous help in my kitchen. Use it to make ice cream. Bread. Nut butter. Salad dressing. Gravy. Cake. Hot soup. Everything.

Food processor

A few of the Life and Health team members and I once attended a raw cooking class led by Chef Ron Russell, of award-winning organic vegan restaurant SunCafe in Los Angeles, California. Minutes into the class, he explained what he considers to be the two most important tools in his kitchen: a high-speed blender (a VitaMix in his case) and a food processor.

You might wonder about the difference between the two (I mean, I just lauded the high-speed blender as being capable of just about everything). Chef Russell explained that

high-speed blenders are wonderful for smooth textures like ice cream, dough, soup, etc. But the food processor is indispensable for the other consistencies, like chunky, minced, diced, etc. You may want to take this into consideration the next time you're chopping (and likely tearing up over) half a dozen onions by hand.

Cutting board

There are all kinds of conflicting advice on cutting boards: which is the most green, the most sanitary, the least damaging to knives, etc. I'll just tell you my personal preference and why.

I have a penchant for my Japanese bamboo cutting board. Because bamboo is a hard grass, it's a sustainable and renewable resource that requires no chemicals to grow or in the harvesting process, making it the choice of many environmentalists. Its hardness also makes it less susceptible to scarring and grooves from constant knife use. The decreased likelihood of knife scarring means that less liquid will seep into the board; lots of people believe that bamboo boards resist bacteria as much or more than regular wooden boards.

My tip: Just make sure to buy one that uses formaldehyde-free glue.

Cookware

The basic cookware you'll need:

SMALL TWO- TO THREE-QUART SAUCEPAN WITH A LID: Use it for boiling or steaming vegetables, making sauces, or cooking grains and pastas.

LARGE FOUR-QUART TO TWO-GALLON SAUCEPAN OR POT WITH A LID: Use this for making pasta sauces, vegetable stocks, or large pots of soup.

MEDIUM TEN- TO FOURTEEN-INCH SKILLET WITH A LID: Perfect for quick cooking techniques like stir-frying.

MEDIUM TEN-INCH NONSTICK PAN: Not to be used over high heat, definitely to be used for smiley face pancakes and tofu scrambles.

MEDIUM FIVE- TO SIX-QUART DUTCH OVEN: A heavy metal pot with thick walls and a lid, Dutch ovens are essential for slow cooking techniques, like braising and even bread baking.

When it comes to cookware material, I prefer stainless steel pots and pans because stainless steel is "nonreactive" (meaning you can cook any kind of food in it), heavy, durable, dishwasher safe, and inexpensive for basic models.

Cooking tools

The basics: essential prep tools and utensils you'll need in your kitchen. For all the following, I generally favor stainless steel and glass over plastic because they're higher quality and infinitely more durable (and I think that balances out the higher cost), but just buy the best quality you can afford.

KNIVES: A good chef's knife is absolutely paramount; an experienced cook (quite possibly you!) will feel like their knife is almost an extension of their arm. But there seems to be an exaggerated hubbub around which chef's knife is best. Stainless versus carbon steel? Stamped versus forged? Japanese? Just start with the three bare essentials (and remember to keep your knives sharpened!):

- Eight- to ten-inch chef's knife: For chopping herbs, vegetables, greens, etc.

- Paring knife: For trimming vegetables and other tasks that require a delicate, precise touch.

- Serrated knife: For slicing bread and other flexible-surface foods like tomatoes.

MEASURING SPOONS: For measuring spices and small qualities. Make sure the spoons are clearly marked so you don't confuse a teaspoon with a tablespoon.

MEASURING CUPS: Standard cup sizes for dry ingredient measurements include ¼, ⅓, ½, ⅔, ¾, and 1 cup sizes. Look for measuring cups with long handles and wide, shallow bodies. Liquid ingredient measuring cups aren't required, per se, but they're specially calibrated for measuring liquids, which differs from measuring dry ingredients. If you can purchase these, make sure there's a spout for pouring, clear measurement markings, and a sturdy handle.

THREE MIXING BOWLS: Small, medium, and large. A very large one is great for general mixing and baking, while a small-to-medium size is needed for mixing dry ingredients. I prefer stainless steel.

WOODEN SPOONS: Endlessly useful, long-lasting if you take care of them properly, and versatile. A few sturdy wooden spoons are essential in any kitchen.

VEGETABLE PEELER: This tool will be in heavy rotation, especially within the context of our cookbook and if you cook often from scratch.

COLANDER OR FINE-MESH STRAINER: For rinsing fruits and vegetables, dumping out pasta, and, well, straining things!

CAN OPENER: Pretty self-explanatory, unless you prefer hacking into your cans with a knife...which I don't recommend.

TOOLS THAT ARE NICE TO HAVE AROUND

Mandoline slicer

This speeds prep work in my kitchen like no other tool or gadget. It slices, minces, and juliennes potatoes, carrots, beets, onions, etc. (Just watch your fingers!)

Garlic press

If you love fifteen cloves of garlic in your stews and roasts, let me introduce you to the garlic press. A little secret: it's also great for juicing tiny citrus.

Slow cooker

It's bulky and takes up precious cabinet space, but I'll never get rid of my slow cooker. It can be such a lifesaver those weeks when time is scarce and I just want to make a big batch of something to see my family through the week. No matter what brand of slow cooker you own, the basics of how to use it are the same: put the ingredient(s) in the cooker, set the cooking, set cooking time, and let it cook.

AN INTERESTING TIP: you can make oatmeal, baked potatoes, applesauce, steamed artichokes, baked apples, brownies, and even bread in a slow cooker!

Salad spinner

They're big and bulky for most small kitchens, but washing and drying greens for salad can feel like a chore at times, and if there's one thing that ruins a salad, it's limp, soggy leaves. Fresh, crisp salad is worth the big spinner.

Rice steamer/rice cooker

Before you knock this off your list, did you know you can make oats, risotto, polenta, and beans in a rice cooker?

Don't let the name fool you; a "rice cooker" might seem like a unitasker, which isn't necessarily a bad thing if you eat a lot of rice. But it can also serve many other purposes, whether you're stuck in a kitchenless studio, need an extra "burner," or just want the convenience of making dishes that require minimal supervision.

Plus, a pot of brown rice is the perfect grain to have around on any given night.

Steamer basket

For steaming vegetables. Make sure it's an adjustable basket so you can fit it in a variety of pot sizes.

TOOLS THAT ARE JUST REALLY COOL

Stand mixer (KitchenAid or Bosch)

If you like to bake or prepare homemade pasta, a stand mixer like the KitchenAid mixer might be worth the splurge. Consider whether or not you have counter space for one (they're big and too heavy to move frequently), if you'd use it more than once a week, and, of course, if you can afford it.

Champion juicer

Yes, the Champion juicer specifically. Not only does it makes a fresh glass of juice quickly, but it also extracts all of the liquid from the fruit or vegetable so you won't be wasting anything. The pulp comes out very dry. Even better: it makes sorbets, nut butters, and non-dairy milks like a dream.

PART THREE *the challenge*

This Book 3.1

This book is as much a cookbook as it is a gentle suggestion. The Life and Health team who produced this book so want you to experience the lightness and freedom of simple, fresh-tasting food. We want to help you as much as we can through these pages.

So, as the word-heavy part of this book comes to a close, bear with me as we give just one more piece of advice. Take a look at the "21-Day Vegan Challenge" we put together using the recipes in this book. Don't worry, we kept your time and money in mind; the recipes in the meal plans are the simplest to prepare and are organized according to similar ingredients.

WHY DO WE FEEL THAT A MEAL PLAN IS SO IMPORTANT?

Life is busy. Your life is moving constantly—whether you're driving to work and preparing the day's mental checklist, sitting in front of your computer and a looming deadline, rushing out for a quick bite of lunch, coming home too mentally drained to focus on preparing a well-balanced dinner. The worst part is, we probably just painted a picture of a day that meets your expectations. Factor in the email you forgot to

The Life and Health team who produced this book so want you to experience the lightness and freedom of simple, fresh-tasting food.

send to your boss and the last-minute errands you have to run before you can go home. That sounds more like it, doesn't it?

All of it is enough to make you feel quite ungrounded and overwhelmed. Enter: **meal plan**. Something small that is, in fact, quite powerful. Let your body take rest in good nutrition.

Fresh. Simple. Balanced. It's our cookbook's identity. At this point, we hope you see that this identity spreads far beyond just what's on your plate, but it's a wonderful place to begin.

QR Codes, How We Can Help

Here's how we can help you as you try your hand at changing your life through good nutrition. When you flip through the recipes, you'll notice a little box like the one on the left under several of them. These little boxes are called "QR codes," which stands for "quick response"—it's basically a two-dimensional barcode. You may have noticed these codes on advertisements, magazines, and bus terminals. But a cookbook? That's right, we're taking this innovative piece of technology a big leap further.

In this cookbook's case, many (but not all) of the QR codes will contain a link to a video demonstrating how to cook a given recipe. We filmed many of the recipes as they were being made, adding written ingredients and instructions to each video to make it as easy as possible for you to cook successfully. Each video is short and sweet and worth the minute or two it takes to learn how to use a QR code. See instructions below and get cookin'!

1. Use your smartphone or tablet to download a free QR code reader app. There should be many options to choose from in your app store. (The "Scan" app is a personal favorite.)

2. Launch the application.

3. Scan the QR code. The app will explain how to do this.

4. Use the video like an animated, easy-to-follow recipe!

All videos found in this book can also be accessed by going to **www.lifeandhealth.org** and searching for the recipe under the recipes tab.

The 21-Day Vegan Challenge WEEK 1

	Sun.	Mon.	Tues.	Wed.	Thurs.	Fri.	Sat.
Breakfast	**Blueberry -Oatmeal Pancakes** (p. 76) + bowl of fruit	**Loaded Toast** (p. 80) + bowl of fruit	**Granola & Milk** (p. 96, 98) + bowl of fruit	**Avocado Toast** (p. 81) + bowl of fruit	**Savory Breakfast Quesadilla** (p. 86) + bowl of fruit	**Sweet Polenta Bowl** (p. 94) + bowl of fruit	**Oatmeal Bake** (p. 93) + non-dairy milk + bowl of fruit
Lunch	**Tofu-Basil Lasagna** (p. 116) + salad	**Italian White Bean Soup** (p. 186) + salad	**Bean & Chili Quesadillas** (p. 151) **Tomato-Avocado Salsa** (p. 254) + fruit	Leftover **Oat Burger** (p. 143) + fruit	**Simple Tofu Salad Sandwich** (p. 148) + fruit	"Sloppy Joe" with left-over **Spicy 3-Bean Chili** (p. 190) + bread + salad	**Sweet Baked Lentils** (p. 224) + brown rice + salad
Dinner	**Oat Burger** (p. 143) + fruit smoothie	Leftover **Tofu-Basil Lasagna** (p. 116) + salad	**Ewald Wild Rice Soup** (p. 194) + salad	**Fresh Tomato-Basil Focaccia** (p. 126) + salad	**Spicy 3-Bean Chili** (p. 190) + bread + salad	**Mujadd-ara** (p. 134) + salad	**Slow-Cooker Sweet Potato Tacos** (p. 121) + fruit
To Do	· *Make either granola recipe* · *Freeze leftover burgers* · *Make salad dressing:* **Lemon -Garlic Vinaigrette**					*Make extra* **brown rice** *and* **lentils** *for Saturday's lunch*	

The 21-Day Vegan Challenge WEEK 2

	Sun.	Mon.	Tues.	Wed.	Thurs.	Fri.	Sat.
Breakfast	French Toast (p. 68) +Strawberry Fields Smoothie (p. 103)	Sweet & Salty Oat Scones (p. 89) + bowl of fruit	Sweet Breakfast Quesadillas (p. 86) + bowl of fruit	Loaded Toast (p. 80) + bowl of fruit	Granola (p. 96, 98) + non-dairy milk + bowl of fruit	10-Minute "Banana Bread" (p. 88) + bowl of fruit	Breakfast Quinoa Bowl (p. 85) + toast + bowl of fruit
Lunch	Baked Falafel (p. 146) + **Tabbouleh** (p. 167) + pita bread + hummus or tzatziki	Hummus Wrap (p. 152) + fruit	Leftover **Creamy Potato Soup** (p. 182) + salad	Mock Tuna Salad Sandwich (p. 150) + fruit	Leftover **Southwest Black Bean Burger** crumbled over salad greens + **Thousand Island Dressing** (p. 264) + fruit	Curried Tofu Salad (p. 149) + bread + leftover salad	Thai Curry Soup (p. 180) + brown rice + salad
Dinner	Kenyan Beans & Rice (p. 128) + salad	Creamy Potato Soup (p. 182) + salad	Asian Tofu Fajitas (p. 108) + fruit salad	Southwest Black Bean Burger (p. 144) + **Chilled Summer Yams** (p. 218)	Caramelized Korean Tofu (p. 216) + brown rice + salad	Pasta Primavera (p. 124) + fruit	Caribbean Burritos with Mango-Lime Salsa (p. 112) + fruit salad
To Do	• Make either **granola** recipe • Prep **Oat Scone** mixture • Make salad dressings: **Orange-Agave, Thousand Island**		Make and refrigerate **Chilled Summer Yams** for Wednesday's dinner		Make enough **brown rice** for Saturday's lunch		

The 21-Day Vegan Challenge WEEK 3

	Sun.	Mon.	Tues.	Wed.	Thurs.	Fri.	Sat.
Breakfast	Cashew-Date Waffles (p. 64) + bowl of fruit	Over-night Oats (p. 90) + bowl of fruit	Loaded Toast (p. 80) + bowl of fruit	Granola (p. 96, 98) + non-dairy milk + bowl of fruit	Savory Breakfast Quesadillas (p. 86) + bowl of fruit	Avocado Toast (p. 81) + bowl of fruit	Oatmeal Bake (p. 93) + non-dairy milk + bowl of fruit
Lunch	Fresh Tomato-Basil Focaccia (p. 126) + salad	ALT Sandwich (p. 153) + fruit	Bean & Chili Quesadillas (p. 151) + leftover Cream of Tomato Soup (p. 199) + fruit	Simple Tofu Salad (p. 148) + bread + fruit	Leftover Creamy Potato Soup (p. 182) + salad	Hummus Wrap (p. 152) + fruit	Kale & White Bean Soup (p. 183) + bread + salad
Dinner	Slow Cooker Sweet Potato Tacos (p. 121) + fruit	Grilled Cheese (p. 154) + Cream of Tomato Soup (p. 199)	Quick Personal Pizza (p. 138) + salad	Creamy Potato Soup (p. 182) + bread + salad	Mujaddara (p. 134) + salad	Asian Shiitake, Kale & Rice Bowl (p. 136) + fruit	Sicilian Tomato-Lentil Pasta (p. 131) + salad
To Do	• *Make either* **granola** *recipe* • *Prep* **Over-night Oats** • *Make salad dressings:* **Lemon-Ginger, Thousand Island**					*Make enough* **brown rice** *and* **lentils** *for Friday and Saturday's dinner*	

PART FOUR *the food*

BREAKFAST

CASHEW-DATE WAFFLES

CASHEWS, DATES AND OATS ARE THREE OF THE MOST UBIQUITOUS INGREDIENTS IN THE VEGAN REPERTOIRE. WE COMBINE ALL THREE IN THIS RECIPE TO MAKE THE QUINTESSENTIAL VEGAN WAFFLE.

Makes 6

2½ cups cold water, divided
½ cup raw cashews
2 to 4 Medjool dates, pitted (or 1 tablespoon agave nectar)
½ teaspoon salt
1 teaspoon vanilla extract
2 cups rolled oats

OPTIONAL TOPPINGS: almond butter, fresh berries, sliced bananas, maple syrup

In a high-speed blender, blend 1 cup of water with the cashews until smooth. Then, add the pitted dates, salt, and vanilla extract and blend until smooth. Add the rolled oats and the remaining water, and blend until smooth. Let the mixture sit for 5 minutes before making the first waffle.

Lightly spray PAM or olive oil on the surface of a heated waffle iron and then pour in ⅙ of the mixture. Bake until the waffle is golden to dark brown, approximately 5 minutes. Repeat for all 6 waffles and enjoy with optional toppings.

Per waffle: 179 calories, 7.1g fat (1.4g saturated fat), 0mg cholesterol, 163mg sodium, 24.4g carbs, 3.3g dietary fiber, 2.7g sugar, 5.4g protein

GRAVY ON TOAST

THINK: *BISCUITS & GRAVY.* THEN, THINK: *GRAVY ON TOAST? THAT'S MUCH HEALTHIER, I THINK I'LL GO WITH THAT INSTEAD!* TRUST ME, YOU WON'T MISS THE BISCUIT WITH A GOOD SLICE OF ARTISAN BREAD AND THIS THICK, SAVORY NUT GRAVY. IT'S THE KIND OF BREAKFAST THAT WILL WARM YOU UP ON THE CHILLIEST OF WINTER MORNINGS.

Serves 4–6

4-6 slices bread, toasted

GRAVY:

¾ cup water, divided
⅓ cup Brazil nuts
½ tablespoon onion powder
1½ tablespoons cornstarch
½ tablespoon nutritional yeast flakes
¾ tablespoon Bragg Liquid Aminos (or soy sauce)
½ teaspoon salt

Bring ½ cup of water to a boil in a medium saucepan. While waiting for the water to boil, blend the rest of the ingredients (nuts, onion powder, cornstarch, nutritional yeast flakes, Bragg Liquid Aminos, and salt) until smooth in ¼ cup of water. Add the blended mixture to the saucepan with the boiling water. Stir over low heat until thickened.

Pour ¼ cup of the gravy over each piece of toast and serve with an optional sprinkle of smoked paprika.

Per slice with 2 tablespoons of gravy: 210 calories, 9g fat (1.7g saturated fat), 0mg cholesterol, 226mg sodium, 37g carbs, 7g dietary fiber, 2g sugar, 4g protein

FRENCH TOAST

A LIGHTER AND COMPLETELY UNIQUE SPIN ON THE CLASSICALLY HEAVIER EGGS AND CREAM FRENCH TOAST (BUT STILL LOOKS AND TASTES LIKE THE REAL THING!).

Serves 6

1 loaf whole-wheat bread, frozen and sliced into twelve ¾-inch slices (whole-wheat sourdough preferred)
1 cup unsweetened soy or almond milk
2 tablespoons cornstarch
¼ cup chickpea flour
½ teaspoon pure vanilla extract

Pour milk in a wide shallow bowl, then mix in the cornstarch and stir until dissolved. Add the chickpea flour and mix until it's mostly absorbed (some lumps are okay).

Heat a nonstick pan or skillet over medium heat and lightly spray the bottom with nonstick spray. Soak the frozen slices of bread in the milk and cornstarch mixture and transfer to the pan. Cook until the toast is golden brown on both sides and serve immediately with maple syrup and a bowl of fresh fruit.

Per slice: 92 calories, 1g fat (0g saturated fat), 0mg cholesterol, 145mg sodium, 17g carbs, 2g dietary fiber, 1g sugar, 4g protein

OVEN-BAKED HASH BROWNS

CRISPY-CRUNCHY AND A PERFECT ACCOMPANIMENT TO ANY SIT-DOWN BREAKFAST. IF YOU DON'T HAVE THE TIME TO PEEL AND SHRED POTATOES, GET A BAG OF FROZEN, PRESHREDDED HASH BROWNS AT YOUR LOCAL MARKET. THANKS TO NEVA BRACKETT FOR THIS RECIPE!

Serves 5–6

1 pound russet potatoes (about 4 potatoes), peeled and shredded
¼ white onion (½ cup), diced finely
¼ cup raw cashews
⅓ cup water
1 tablespoon McKay's Chicken Style Instant Broth and Seasoning (or other chicken-like seasoning)
½ tablespoon onion powder
½ teaspoon garlic powder

Preheat the oven to 400°F. Peel the potatoes and use a mandolin to shred them. Add the cashews, water, McKay's seasoning, onion powder, and garlic powder to a high-speed blender and blend until smooth. Combine the mixture with the diced onions and shredded potatoes and mix.

Place everything on a nonstick cookie sheet and bake until the edges are golden brown, about 20 minutes.

Per 1-cup serving: 106 calories, 3.3g fat (0.7g saturated fat), 0mg cholesterol, 391mg sodium, 17.4g carbs, 2.5g dietary fiber, 1.8g sugar, 2.7g protein

SIMPLE SCRAMBLED TOFU

ALL IT TAKES IS A PINCH OF TURMERIC FOR TOFU TO TAKE ON THE SAME COLOR AS EGGS! MAKE THE BASE SCRAMBLE AND STIR IN AS MANY OR AS FEW OF THE SUGGESTED ADD-INS TO CREATE YOUR OWN PERFECT TOFU SCRAMBLE RECIPE.

Serves 2–4

1 package medium firm tofu, drained
1 clove garlic, minced
1 tablespoon low-sodium soy sauce
½ teaspoon turmeric
1 teaspoon butter-flavored salt (optional, for an "eggier" flavor)

PRESS THE EXCESS WATER OUT OF THE TOFU: Place tofu on a flat surface and lay a dry dishtowel on top of the tofu. Gently press down on the towel with your hands or a heavy book to remove any the water.

In a pan over medium heat, sauté the garlic with optional vegetables and a little water. Crumble the tofu with your hands into the pan. Add the soy sauce, turmeric, and butter-flavored salt. Sauté the mixture until heated through and the tofu is evenly coated.

OPTIONAL VEGETABLE ADD-INS:

chopped tomatoes
broccoli florets
cubed zucchini
diced red, orange, and/or yellow bell peppers
chopped spinach
sliced carrots
cauliflower florets
sliced mushrooms
diced onions
additional minced garlic

OPTIONAL HERB ADD-INS:

cilantro
parsley
basil
oregano

OPTIONAL SPICE ADD-INS:

cumin
cayenne
Creole seasoning

Per 1-cup serving: 113 calories, 6.4g fat (1.3g saturated fat), 0mg cholesterol, 319mg sodium, 3.8g carbs, 1.6g dietary fiber, 1g sugar, 12.8g protein

SIMPLE PANCAKES

MY FAMILY LOVES THESE LIGHT AND FLUFFY PANCAKES EXACTLY THE WAY THIS COOKBOOK SHOWS: WITH A LITTLE DAB OF ALMOND BUTTER AND SLICED BANANAS.

Makes 6

¾ cup whole-wheat flour
¾ cup all-purpose flour
1 tablespoon baking powder
½ teaspoon salt
2 tablespoons agave nectar
1 flax egg (1 tablespoon ground flaxseed + 3 tablespoons water)
1 tablespoon water
1 ½ cup unsweetened soy or almond milk

Make the flax egg by mixing 1 tablespoon ground flax with 3 tablespoons of water and letting it sit for 10 minutes. The consistency should resemble that of an egg.

Combine the dry ingredients (whole-wheat flour, white flour, baking powder, salt) and mix well. When the dry ingredients are well incorporated, add the liquid ingredients (agave nectar, flax egg, water, and milk). Stir the ingredients gently and no more than necessary, just enough to combine. This is done in order to prevent the baking powder from becoming active and resulting in a very thin pancake.

Pour ½-cup rounds of the batter onto a heated griddle or pan over medium heat and cook for about 3 minutes. When the edges start to bubble, flip the pancakes over and cook until the other side is golden brown.

NOTE: While mixing the batter, more water may be necessary to reach the desired consistency.

Per pancake: 157 calories, 2g fat (0.2g saturated fat), 0mg cholesterol, 463mg sodium, 31g carbs, 3g dietary fiber, 7g sugar, 5g protein

BLUEBERRY-OATMEAL PANCAKES

DUE TO THE ADDITION OF OATS IN THIS RECIPE, THESE PANCAKES ARE A LITTLE DENSER AND HEARTIER THAN THE **SIMPLE PANCAKES** (P.75). MAKE A BIG STEAMING STACK AND SERVE THEM WITH A MUG OF WARM TEA FOR A COZY WINTER BREAKFAST.

Makes 6

1 cup rolled oats
1 cup unsweetened soy or almond milk
2 flax eggs (2 tablespoons ground flaxseed + 6 tablespoons water)
2 tablespoons canola oil
½ cup all-purpose flour
½ teaspoon baking soda
½ teaspoon baking powder
2 tablespoons granulated sugar
½ teaspoon salt
3 tablespoons oat bran
1 cup fresh or frozen blueberries (optional)

Make the flax egg by mixing the ground flax with 6 tablespoons of water and letting it sit for 10 minutes. The consistency should resemble that of an egg.

In a bowl, mix together the oats, milk, flax eggs, and oil. In a small separate bowl, mix the flour, baking soda, baking powder, sugar, and salt. Then combine both mixtures and stir, adding more milk if necessary for your desired consistency.

Lightly grease a hot skillet or pan with additional oil. Pour ½-cup pancake rounds on the skillet and cook until bubbles form on the surface. Carefully drop 6–8 optional blueberries onto one side of each pancake, then flip and cook on the other side until golden brown.

Per pancake: 172 calories, 7g fat (0.5g saturated fat), 0mg cholesterol, 356mg sodium, 23g carbs, 2g dietary fiber, 6g sugar, 4g protein

OVERNIGHT CHIA-OAT PUDDING

CHIA SEEDS ARE FASCINATING LITTLE BUNDLES OF OMEGA-3S. WHEN THEY'RE SOAKED IN WATER, A GELATINOUS COATING FORMS AROUND THE SEED, VERY MUCH LIKE TOMATO SEEDS. I LIKE MASHED BANANA IN THIS BECAUSE IT THICKENS THE MIXTURE WHILE ADDING A LOT OF VOLUME. IF THE PUDDING IS TOO THIN FOR YOUR LIKING, YOU CAN ADD MORE CHIA SEEDS AND LET IT SIT FOR 10 MORE MINUTES.

Serves 1

⅓ cup rolled oats
1 cup unsweetened soy or almond milk
1 tablespoon chia seeds
1 overripe banana, mashed
¼ teaspoon pure vanilla extract
pinch of salt

Recipe for pictured berry cream can be found in **Neapolitan Chia-Banana Parfait** (p.231)

Mix ingredients in a bowl and place in the fridge overnight. In the morning, add your choice of toppings such as sliced peaches, mangoes, berries, a dab of nut butter—whatever you'd like.

TIP: If you're not a fan of the tapioca-like consistency of chia seed pudding, transfer pudding to a blender and blend until smooth.

Per 1-cup serving: 280 calories, 8.2g fat (0.6g saturated fat), 0mg cholesterol, 417mg sodium, 50.5g carbs, 9.3g dietary fiber, 14.8g sugar, 7.4g protein

LOADED TOAST

THE ONLY KNIFE-AND-FORK TOAST YOU'LL EVER EAT.

Serves 1–2

2 slices whole-grain bread, about 1-inch thick each
1 tablespoon peanut or almond butter
1 banana, sliced into ¼-inch coins
½ cup unsweetened applesauce, warmed or cold
mixed nuts, chopped (optional)

Toast bread. While the bread is toasting, warm the applesauce on the stovetop or the microwave. Once the toast is ready, spread ½ tablespoon of almond butter on each slice, layering banana slices, then applesauce on top. Garnish with nuts for additional crunch.

Per slice: 220 calories, 5.2g fat (0.5g saturated fat), 0mg cholesterol, 127mg sodium, 37.8g carbs, 7.6g dietary fiber, 16.5g sugar, 6.4g protein

AVOCADO TOAST

WE'VE NICKNAMED THIS "THE BEST AVOCADO TOAST YOU'LL EVER HAVE." IF YOU'RE FOLLOWING OUR 21-DAY VEGAN CHALLENGE (P. 57), YOU'LL SOON SEE WHY. THE LITTLE DETAILS MAKE IT "THE BEST" TITLE COMES FROM LITTLE DETAILS LIKE SUPER CRUSTY AND SEEDY TOAST, PERFECTLY RIPE AVOCADO, TANGY LIME, AND A BONUS BLACK BEAN PROTEIN BOOST.

Serves 2

4 thick slices of multi-grain bread
1 ripe avocado
pinch of salt
¼ lime, juiced (1 teaspoon)
1 large tomato, sliced (optional)
½ cup black beans, warmed (optional)

Pit the avocado, then scoop the flesh out of the skin into a small bowl. Sprinkle on salt, then spritz with the lime. Mash with a fork (mash well to create a smooth spread, or mash just a few times to create a chunky spread). Toast the bread, then spread the avocado on each slice, adding sliced tomato and/or a spoonful of black beans on top for added protein.

Per 2-slice serving: 300 calories, 16.9g fat (2.6g saturated fat), 0mg cholesterol, 343mg sodium, 31.8g carbs, 10.6g dietary fiber, 4.1g sugar, 9g protein

ROASTED HERB POTATOES

A LITTLE ROASTING GOES A LONG WAY, ESPECIALLY WHEN YOU HAVE THE PERFECT COMBINATION OF WAXY RED POTATOES AND HERBS. DON'T LIMIT THESE TO ONLY BREAKFAST; THEY'D MAKE A PERFECTLY DECENT SIDE DISH FOR ANY OF OUR ENTRÉES.

Serves 4–6

3 pounds small red potatoes, halved widthwise
1 medium yellow onion, quartered and sliced ½-inch thick
1 tablespoon extra-virgin olive oil
coarse salt, to taste
4 teaspoons fresh rosemary, chopped (or 1 teaspoon dried rosemary)
4 teaspoons fresh thyme, chopped (or 1 teaspoon dried thyme)

OPTIONAL FLAVORFUL ADDITIONS:

¼ cup nutritional yeast flakes
¼ teaspoon cayenne pepper
2 teaspoons granulated garlic

Preheat oven to 450°F. Distribute the potatoes and onions evenly on a large rimmed baking sheet. Sprinkle with oil and salt, and then toss to coat (it helps to use your hands for this).

Place in the oven and roast for 35 minutes. After 35 minutes. Remove the potatoes from the oven, sprinkle with herbs, toss to coat, then return to oven and roast for 20 minutes longer. The potatoes should be brown and tender.

Per 1-cup serving: 253 calories, 6.2g fat (1g saturated fat), 0mg cholesterol, 65mg sodium, 46.4g carbs, 4.8g dietary fiber, 3.6g sugar, 5.5g protein

BREAKFAST QUINOA BOWL

QUINOA IS A WONDERFUL, WONDERFUL SEED AND COMPLETE PROTEIN, WHICH MEANS IT CONTAINS ALL NINE ESSENTIAL AMINO ACIDS. MOST PEOPLE TEND TO ADD QUINOA TO A SAVORY LUNCH OR DINNER, BUT WE'RE TURNING THAT ON ITS HEAD BY COMBINING QUINOA WITH SWEET INGREDIENTS FOR A HEALTHY BREAKFAST.

Serves 2–4

2 cups vanilla or unsweetened soy or almond milk
1 cup quinoa, rinsed
2 tablespoons agave nectar
Pinch of ground cinnamon
1 cup mixed fresh or frozen berries

OPTIONAL ADD-INS: additional berries, additional milk, agave, and cinnamon

In a small saucepan, bring milk to a boil. Add the quinoa to the milk and return to a boil. Reduce the heat to a simmer and cover until ¾ of the milk has been absorbed, approximately 10 minutes.

Stir in the agave nectar and cinnamon and cook, covered, until almost all the milk is absorbed—about 5 minutes. Stir in the berries and cook for 30 seconds. Serve with additional milk, agave, cinnamon, and berries.

Per 1-cup serving: 491 calories, 9g fat (0.5 saturated fat), 0mg cholesterol, 105mg sodium, 86g carbs, 10g dietary fiber, 17g sugar, 21g protein

SWEET OR SAVORY BREAKFAST QUESADILLAS

WEEKEND MORNINGS ARE SPECIAL, A CHANCE TO TAKE MY TIME MAKING BREAKFAST. SOMETIMES, THOUGH, I DON'T WANT TO LINGER OVER THE COOKING. ENTER THE VERY SPECIAL AND QUICK-COOKING BREAKFAST QUESADILLA; DRESSED UP OR DOWN WITH WHICHEVER SWEET OR SAVORY INGREDIENTS YOU HAVE ON HAND. THESE ARE A WONDERFUL AND COLORFUL BREAK FROM THE SPEEDY TOAST AND OATMEAL ROUTINE OF TYPICAL MONDAY—FRIDAY MORNINGS.

1 quesadilla = 1 serving

One 10" whole-grain tortilla

SWEET: whole-grain tortillas + nut butter + bananas + berries

SAVORY: whole-grain tortillas + hummus + mashed black beans + salsa + avocado

Begin by spreading the base (almond butter or hummus) on the entire tortilla, then layer the rest of the sweet or savory ingredients onto half the tortilla. Fold the tortilla in half over the fillings, then toast in a pan without oil over medium heat until the outsides are slightly crunchy. Cut into wedges and serve.

SWEET: *per quesadilla: 281 calories, 10.4g fat (0.9g saturated fat), 0mg cholesterol, 130mg sodium, 42.5g carbs, 6.4g dietary fiber, 9.7g sugar, 8.3g protein*

SAVORY: *per quesadilla: 333 calories, 9.2g fat (0.9g saturated fat), 0mg cholesterol, 185mg sodium, 48.4g carbs, 17.2g dietary fiber, 1.7g sugar, 20.3g protein*

10-MINUTE BANANA BREAD

IT DOESN'T READ OR LOOK LIKE TYPICAL BANANA BREAD, BUT IT TASTES SURPRISINGLY SIMILAR TO THE CLASSIC. IF YOUR FAVORITE BANANA BREAD RECIPE HAS WALNUTS IN IT, TRY SPRINKLING SOME ON TOP AFTER THE BREAD COMES OUT OF THE OVEN.

Serves 1–2

½ overripe banana
1 tablespoon almond butter
2 slices whole-grain bread
½ teaspoon ground cinnamon
pure maple syrup, for topping (optional)
chopped walnuts, for topping (optional)

Preheat toaster oven to 375°F. Mash the banana with the almond butter, then mix in the cinnamon. Spread the mixture over 2 slices of bread, sprinkling extra cinnamon on top (optional). Bake the 2 pieces of bread for 10 minutes. Once baked, drizzle with maple syrup and sprinkle with chopped walnuts.

Per slice: 287 calories, 11.2g fat (1.4g saturated fat), 0mg cholesterol, 301mg sodium, 42.2g carbs, 6.8g dietary fiber, 11.3g sugar, 10.1g protein

SWEET & SALTY OAT SCONES

THESE LITTLE ROUND SCONES ARE A SOFTER AND CHEWIER ADAPTATION OF OATCAKES, TRADITIONAL SCOTTISH HARD CRACKERS OR BISCUITS THAT ARE SERVED WITH JAM, DIP, OR ON THEIR OWN.

Makes 8–10

¼ cup whole-wheat flour
1 cup unsalted mixed nuts
1 cup rolled oats
1 teaspoon vanilla extract
¼ cup agave nectar, warmed
1 teaspoon salt
¼ cup dried cranberries (or raisins), chopped

Preheat the oven to 350°F. Place the flour and nuts into a food processor or blender and blend until the mixture reaches a flour-like consistency. Be careful not to blend too much, otherwise it'll turn into nut butter. Transfer to a large mixing bowl.

Add the remaining ingredients until the mixture sticks together (you may need to add a tablespoon or so of water). Divide into 9 balls and place on an oiled baking sheet. Press down gently on each ball until it's about 2½ inches wide. Bake for 8 minutes, then use a spatula to flip the cakes and bake for an additional 6 minutes.

Per 2-scone serving: 314 calories, 17.3g fat (2.8g saturated fat), 0mg cholesterol, 464mg sodium, 35.9g carbs, 4.4g dietary fiber, 13.8g sugar, 7.3g protein

SIMPLE OVERNIGHT OATS

THIS IS ONE OF MY FAVORITE WAYS TO HAVE OATMEAL. TOSS THE INGREDIENTS TOGETHER THE NIGHT BEFORE AND IT'LL BE READY TO GO IN THE MORNING.

Serves 4

2 cups rolled oats
2 cups unsweetened almond or soy milk
⅓ cup agave nectar
3 tablespoons ground flaxseed (or whole chia seeds)
1 teaspoon ground cinnamon
2 ripe bananas, chopped
pinch of salt
1 teaspoon pure vanilla extract

OPTIONAL MIX-INS: blueberries, chopped nuts

In a large bowl, mix all ingredients together, including the optional mix-ins. Cover and leave in the fridge overnight, or at least 2 hours. Give it a stir in the morning and serve cold with granola and additional berries and nuts on top.

Can keep in the fridge for 2–3 days.

Per 1-cup serving: 259 calories, 5.6g fat (0.7g saturated), 0mg cholesterol, 134mg sodium, 44.4g carbs, 8.1g dietary fiber, 9.5g sugar, 7.3g protein

OATMEAL BAKE

THIS PUSHES ALL OF THE BUTTONS THAT BREAKFAST SHOULD PUSH: IT'S SWEET BUT NOT TOO SWEET, FILLING BUT NOT TOO FILLING, AND THE LEFTOVERS MIGHT BECOME YOUR FAVORITE SNACK, WHETHER HOT, ROOM TEMPERATURE, OR COLD.

Serves 6–8

2 cups rolled oats
1 (8-ounce) can crushed pineapple
½ cup mixed nuts, coarsely chopped
1 teaspoon vanilla extract
½ teaspoon salt
1½ cups apple juice
2 cups fresh or frozen mixed berries

Preheat the oven to 350°F. Mix together all of the ingredients, then bake for 30 minutes. Pour a splash of milk on top and serve with additional berries.

Per 1-cup serving: 182 calories, 6.6g fat (1.1g saturated fat), 0mg cholesterol, 147mg sodium, 27.9g carbs, 4.2g dietary fiber, 9.9g sugar, 4.5g protein

5-MINUTE SWEET OR SAVORY POLENTA BOWL

THIS IS A SINGLE SERVING RECIPE, BUT HOW PERFECT WOULD THIS BE FOR A UNIQUE BRUNCH BUFFET? JUST PREPARE THE POLENTA AND LAY OUT THE OPTIONAL TOPPINGS FOR A BEAUTIFUL, CUSTOMIZABLE, AND SUNSHINE-Y SPREAD.

Serves 1

1 cup water
¼ cup cornmeal, coarsely ground
1 teaspoon extra-virgin olive oil
pinch of salt (optional)
splash of unsweetened almond or soy milk (optional)

SWEET TOPPINGS: fresh or dried fruit, pure maple syrup, toasted nuts, granola

SAVORY TOPPINGS: sautéed mushrooms, onions, cherry tomatoes, fresh herbs

In a microwaveable bowl, mix the water, cornmeal, oil, and salt. Place the bowl, uncovered, in the microwave and heat on high for 5 minutes. Halfway through cooking, take the bowl out of the microwave and give it a stir, adding a splash of milk if the polenta looks like it's drying out. Put the bowl back in the microwave and heat the rest of the time. It should be thick and will thicken more as it cools.

Eat with sweet or savory toppings, or plain.

Per recipe (without toppings): 150 calories, 5.8g fat (0.8g saturated fat), 0mg cholesterol, 173mg sodium, 23.4g carbs, 2.2g dietary fiber, 2.5g protein

LARGE-BATCH DATE & NUT GRANOLA

WHY SUCH A LARGE BATCH? MY FAMILY OF FIVE CAN EAT AND ENJOY AN ASTONISHING AMOUNT OF GRANOLA FOR BREAKFAST. PLUS, WHAT IS GRANOLA BUT A PERFECT BREAKFAST FOOD, GARNISH, AND EVERYDAY SNACK?

Serves about 30

½ cup pure maple syrup
½ cup agave nectar
¼ cup molasses
1½ cups Medjool dates, pitted
1 cup nuts of choice
15 cups rolled oats
1 cup raw almonds, coarsely ground
1 cup raw walnuts or pecans, coarsely ground
1 cup raw sunflower seeds
1 cup raw pumpkin seeds
1 tablespoon vanilla extract
1 teaspoon salt

Preheat the oven to 180°F. Add the agave nectar, maple syrup, molasses, dates, and 1 cup of your preferred nuts to a high-speed blender and blend until smooth. Add the wet mixture to the oats, and then add the rest of the ingredients, mixing them together with a wooden spoon until the oats are covered with the mixture evenly on.

Spread the mixture out evenly on multiple baking sheets, about ½-inch thick throughout. Bake in the oven for 8 hours, or until golden brown.

Per ½-cup serving: 369 calories, 14.2g fat (1.9g saturated fat), 0mg cholesterol, 79mg sodium, 53.6g carbs, 7.8g dietary fiber, 14.7g sugar, 10.4g protein

QUICK CHIA-NUT GRANOLA

IT'S DANGEROUS TO HAVE CRUNCHY, FRESHLY BAKED GRANOLA SITTING ON THE COUNTER WITHIN ARM'S REACH. THIS IS A SMALL BATCH, SO EXERCISE YOUR WILLPOWER AND APPEASE YOUR TEMPTATIONS WITH JUST ONE HOT CLUSTER.

Makes 1 quart

2 cups rolled oats
½ cup wheat germ
1 tablespoon dark brown sugar
¼ teaspoon salt
½ cup maple syrup
3 tablespoons extra-virgin olive oil
1 tablespoon water
½ teaspoon vanilla extract
½ tablespoon chia seeds or flaxseed (optional)
½ cup pistachios, roughly chopped (optional)
¼ cup raw almonds, roughly chopped (optional)
½ cup unsweetened coconut flakes (optional)
½ cup dried apricots or cranberries, chopped (optional)

Preheat oven to 275°F. In a large bowl, mix the oats, wheat germ, brown sugar, salt, chia seeds, almonds, and coconut.

Bring the syrup, oil, water, cinnamon, and vanilla to a simmer in a saucepan over low heat. Drizzle the wet mixture over the oat mixture and stir to combine. Working one handful at a time, squeeze the oats to form small clumps and transfer to a nonstick baking pan. It's okay if some of the clumps fall apart.

Bake for 30 minutes, then take the pan out and stir in the dried cranberries. Place back in the oven and continue to bake until the granola is golden brown, about 15 minutes. Let it cool on the counter for 5 minutes or so; it'll become crispier as it cools.

Granola can be stored in an airtight container for up to 2 weeks.

Per ½-cup serving: 216 calories, 9.6g fat (0.9g saturated fat), 0mg cholesterol, 76mg sodium, 28.5g carbs, 4.1g dietary fiber, 7.9g sugar, 5.8g protein

TANGERINE BLISS SMOOTHIE

I WAS TEMPTED TO NAME THIS "TANGERINE JULIUS" BECAUSE OF HOW INTENSELY SIMILAR IT TASTES TO THE POPULAR MALL DRINK "ORANGE JULIUS." IT'S FROTHY, VIVIDLY ORANGE, AND FEELS LIKE YOU'RE DRINKING A GLASS OF SUNSHINE.

Serves 7

5 Medjool dates, pitted
1 cup unsweetened soy or almond milk
1 teaspoon pure vanilla extract
1 tablespoon agave nectar
10 tangerines, peeled
1 tray ice cubes (about 16 cubes)

Place the dates, milk, vanilla extract, and agave nectar in a high-speed blender and blend until smooth. Add the tangerines, then blend until smooth. Finally, add the ice cubes and blend until smooth again.

Per 1-cup serving: 78 calories, 0.7g fat, 0mg cholesterol, 26mg sodium, 18.1g carbs, 3.4g dietary fiber, 14.5g sugar, 1.4g protein

STRAWBERRY FIELDS SMOOTHIE

CREATED BY MY DEAR FRIENDS AND SMOOTHIE WIZARDS ASHLEY KIM AND RACHELLE DIAZ, THIS SMOOTHIE LIVES UP TO ITS NAME IN TASTE, WITH A SURPRISINGLY SUMMERY NOTE FROM THE BASIL.

Serves 4–5

4 cups fresh strawberries
½ cup peaches, frozen
5 leaves fresh basil or mint
1 cup vanilla almond milk
1 teaspoon agave nectar

Place everything in a high-speed blender and blend until smooth.

Per 1-cup serving: 58 calories, 0.6g fat, 0mg cholesterol, 36mg sodium, 11.7g carbs, 2.1g dietary fiber, 8.9g sugar, 1.2g protein

Corn & Green Chile Enchiladas

Asian Tofu Fajitas

Tofu Thai Curry

Caribbean Burritos with Mango-Lime Salsa

Roasted Tomato, Spinach & Basil Pasta

Tofu-Basil Lasagna (left)

Vegetable Pot Pie

Lentil Roast

Slow Cooker Sweet Potato Tacos

Mac & Cheeze

Pasta Primavera

Fresh Tomato-Basil Focaccia

Kenyan Beans & Rice

Sicilian Tomato-Lentil Pasta

Creamy Mushroom Stroganoff

Mujaddara (Lebanese Lentils)

Asian Shiitake, Kale & Rice Bowl

Quick Personal Pizza

Homemade Nachos

Oat Burger

Southwest Black Bean Burger

Baked Falafel

Simple Tofu Salad

Curried Tofu Salad

Mock Tuna Salad

Bean & Green Chile Quesadillas

Hummus Wrap

ALT Sandwich

Grilled Cheese Sandwich

ENTRÉES

CORN & GREEN CHILE ENCHILADAS

DON'T LET THE LENGTH OF THIS RECIPE SCARE YOU—THIS MEETS THE NEEDS OF BOTH THOSE IN A HURRY AND THOSE WHO WANT TO TAKE THEIR TIME. YOU CAN MAKE THESE ENCHILADAS QUICKLY WITH STORE-BOUGHT SAUCE AND MEAT SUBSTITUTE, OR MAKE BOTH AT HOME. EITHER WAY, THESE ENCHILADAS ARE WORTH IT. CREAMY, SLIGHTLY SPICY, AND SKY-HIGH IN FLAVOR THANKS TO THE BULGUR "MEAT," CORN, AND GREEN CHILES, THEY'RE THE PERFECT DISH FOR ANY DINNER TABLE.

Serves 8–10

8 whole-grain or corn tortillas, warmed

2 cups frozen corn, thawed

1 (16-ounce) can black beans, drained and rinsed (or white beans)

½ cup Tofutti sour cream

1 (4-ounce) can diced fire-roasted green chiles

Vegan cheese shreds, such as Daiya Cheddar Style Cheese Shreds, for topping (optional)

ENCHILADA SAUCE (OR 3 CUPS STORE-BOUGHT ENCHILADA SAUCE)

1 (16-ounce) can tomato sauce

2 cups water

½ teaspoon ground cumin

½ teaspoon garlic powder

½ teaspoon onion salt

¼ teaspoon chili powder (add more for spicier flavor)

3 tablespoons whole-wheat flour

1 vegetarian bouillon cube

1 tablespoon fresh lemon juice

½ teaspoon sugar

GROUND BULGUR "MEAT" (P. 204) (OR 2 CUPS STORE-BOUGHT VEGGIE BURGER)

1 cup Ground Bulgur Meat (p. 204)
¼ cup water
1 tablespoon taco seasoning

MAKE THE ENCHILADA SAUCE: Mix all of the ingredients together in a saucepan. Bring to a boil and simmer for 10 minutes.

MAKE THE GROUND BURGER: Add 1 cup of bulgur or veggie meat, water, and taco seasoning to a saucepan. Sauté for a few minutes, then set aside until enchiladas are ready to assemble.

ASSEMBLE THE ENCHILADAS: Preheat the oven to 350°F. In a 9x13 casserole dish, spoon just enough enchilada sauce to coat the bottom, about ½ cup. Soak a tortilla in the pot of sauce and spoon on the beans, corn, burger, green chiles, and sour cream in the center. Roll and place it in the casserole dish. Evenly pour the rest of the sauce over the rolled enchiladas and sprinkle with cheese.

Cover with foil and bake for 30 minutes.

Per enchilada: 250 calories, 6.5g fat (1.5g saturated fat), 0mg cholesterol, 948mg sodium, 45g carbs, 8g dietary fiber, 6g sugar, 8g protein

ASIAN TOFU FAJITAS

I FIRST TASTED THESE ASIAN-INSPIRED FAJITAS AT A FRIEND'S HOUSEWARMING PARTY. MEGHAN MCKINNEY, THE AUTHOR OF THIS RECIPE, SERVED THEM TO US ON PERFECTLY WARMED CORN TORTILLAS AND A LITTLE SCOOP OF BROWN RICE. NEEDLESS TO SAY, THEY WERE A HIT.

Serves 4–6

6-8 whole-grain or corn tortillas, warmed
¼ cup Bragg Liquid Aminos (or low-sodium soy sauce)
¼ cup water
½ tablespoon maple syrup
1 tablespoon nutritional yeast flakes (optional)
¼ teaspoon cayenne pepper
1 tablespoon extra-virgin olive oil
1 (16-ounce) package extra-firm tofu
3 cloves garlic, minced
1 small onion, julienned
2 bell peppers, julienned

Make the sauce by mixing together Bragg Liquid Aminos, water, maple syrup, nutritional yeast, cayenne pepper, and oil. Set aside.

Prepare the tofu by draining the water out of the container and gently squeezing out the excess moisture with a paper towel. Cut into ½-inch matchsticks.

Heat a little olive oil in a shallow pan and add the sliced onions and garlic. When the onions start to become translucent, add the bell peppers.

Meanwhile in a separate nonstick pan, heat a little olive oil and cook the tofu over medium-high heat. Cook the tofu on all sides until slightly browned. Transfer them to the pan with the veggies and pour in the sauce mixture. Simmer for 5 minutes and serve in warm tortillas.

Per fajita: 176 calories, 8g fat (1.1g saturated fat), 0mg cholesterol, 619mg sodium, 19g carbs, 2.7g dietary fiber, 3.3g sugar, 11g protein

TOFU THAI CURRY

THAI RESTAURANTS ARE NEAR AND DEAR TO MANY A VEGAN'S HEART. WHY? USUALLY, IF NOT ALWAYS, A LARGE PORTION OF THEIR MENUS ARE FRIENDLY TO PLANT-BASED DIETS! THIS CURRY RECIPE IS AS CLOSE TO THAI RESTAURANT TASTE AND QUALITY AS I'VE EVER SEEN. IT IS ABSOLUTELY WORTH A TRY. WARM THANKS TO MY GOOD FRIEND SHARON CHO FOR THIS RECIPE!

Serves 6–8

3-6 cups cooked brown rice
1 (16-ounce) package extra firm tofu, drained and cut in ½-inch cubes
1 tablespoon extra-virgin olive oil
1 medium onion, chopped
1 teaspoon ground cumin
1 tablespoon garlic, pressed
1 tablespoon ginger, minced finely
1 teaspoon curry powder
1½ teaspoon salt
1 teaspoon jalapeño pepper, seeded and minced (or 1 teaspoon chili pepper paste*, or more to taste)
1 (14-ounce) can coconut milk
1 (14.5-ounce) can diced tomatoes
1 cup potato, cut in ½-inch cubes
½ cup carrot, cut in ½-inch cubes
½ cup yellow or red bell pepper, julienned
½ cup fresh or frozen peas
8 fresh basil leaves, chopped (or ½ teaspoon dry basil, to taste)

*Chili pepper paste can be found in the Asian section of most supermarkets.

Cook the rice according to package directions. Preheat oven to 375°F to begin baking the tofu. Spray a baking sheet with oil. Lay the tofu cubes out evenly, spray with oil, then sprinkle with salt. Bake for about 20 minutes until golden brown.

While the tofu is baking, prepare the curry. In a pot, sauté the onions and cumin over medium-high heat in olive oil until onions are transparent. Add ginger, garlic, curry powder, salt, and jalapeño pepper. Sauté for a couple of more minutes. Stir in coconut milk, diced tomatoes, potatoes, carrots, and bell pepper. Bring to a simmer for 10 minutes, making sure to stir occasionally.

Add the baked tofu cubes, peas, and basil leaves, and then cover and simmer for about 5 minutes, until the vegetables are tender.

Serve the tofu curry over brown rice and season to taste with hot chili sauce.

Per 1-cup serving (without rice): 276 calories, 20g fat (11g saturated fat), 0mg cholesterol, 767mg sodium, 16g carbs, 3g dietary fiber, 4g sugar, 11g protein

CARIBBEAN BURRITOS WITH MANGO-LIME SALSA

THIS BURRITO RECIPE IS PURE *WOW*, FROM HEAD TO TOE. FRAGRANT COCONUT-CINNAMON RICE, FRESH AND ZINGY MANGO-LIME SALSA, HEARTY BLACK BEANS, AND EXOTIC TOASTED COCONUT FLAKES...YOU GET THE PICTURE. IF YOU'D LIKE TO REDUCE THE CARB CONTENT IN THIS RECIPE, TURN IT INTO A "GRAIN BOWL" BY OMITTING THE TORTILLA AND JUST SPOONING THE BEANS AND SALSA ATOP A PILE OF COCONUT RICE.

Serves 8–10

10 large whole-wheat tortillas
1 (15-ounce) can black beans, drained, rinsed, and heated through
1 cup coconut flakes, toasted

COCONUT RICE:

2 cups uncooked jasmine rice, washed
1 stick cinnamon (optional)
1½ cups water
1 can coconut milk
2 tablespoons sugar
¼ teaspoon salt

MANGO-LIME SALSA:

2 ripe mangoes, peeled, seeded, and diced into ¼-inch cubes
1½ tablespoons jalapeño pepper, seeded and minced
1 tablespoon shallots, minced
¼ cup fresh cilantro, coarsely chopped
2 tablespoons fresh lime juice
½ teaspoon salt

MAKE THE COCONUT RICE: In a saucepan, combine all ingredients and bring to a boil. Cover the pan and reduce the heat to low, allowing the rice to simmer for 20 minutes, or until the rice is fluffy. Remove from heat, stir with a fork, cover, and let sit for 10 minutes. Remove the cinnamon stick before serving.

MAKE THE MANGO-LIME SALSA: In a medium bowl, combine all ingredients. Toss gently and serve.

TOAST THE COCONUT: In a skillet over medium heat, toast the coconut for about 3 minutes, turning frequently with a spatula until browned and toasted on all sides.

ASSEMBLE BURRITOS: Spoon the coconut rice, black beans, and mango-lime salsa into warmed tortillas, then sprinkle the coconut flakes on top. Wrap burritos and serve.

Per burrito: 422 calories, 15g fat (11g saturated fat), 0mg cholesterol, 440mg sodium, 64g carbs, 7g dietary fiber, 15g sugar, 10g protein

ROASTED TOMATO, SPINACH & BASIL PASTA

HIDE TWO BIG HANDFULS OF SPINACH BETWEEN AROMATIC BASIL, SWEET AND JUICY ROASTED TOMATOES, AND LOTS OF SAUTÉED GARLIC. IT'S A PERFECT, PERFECT PLATE OF PASTA.

Serves 4–6

4-5 cups cherry tomatoes, halved
2 tablespoons sun-dried tomatoes, chopped
1 tablespoon extra-virgin olive oil
6 cloves garlic, minced
1 teaspoon salt
2 cups baby spinach, coarsely chopped
8 ounces (½ package) thin whole-wheat spaghetti
½ cup fresh basil, chopped

¼ cup pine nuts, toasted (optional)
1 tablespoon lemon juice (optional)
1 pinch cayenne pepper (optional)

Preheat oven to 400°F. Toss the tomatoes with olive oil, garlic and salt. Spread the coated tomatoes on a foil-lined roasting sheet and roast until the tomatoes are shriveled and lightly browned, approximately 20-30 minutes. Once they have finished roasting, scrape the tomatoes and juices into a large bowl. Add the spinach and sun-dried tomatoes to the bowl.

While the tomatoes are roasting, prepare the pasta according to the package directions. When the pasta is ready, drain it and toss with the spinach, roasted tomatoes, basil, and if so desired, lemon juice and cayenne pepper. To finish, sprinkle with toasted pine nuts and serve.

Per 1-cup serving: 270 calories, 6g fat (0.6g saturated fat), 0mg cholesterol, 623mg sodium, 54g carbs, 8g dietary fiber, 0.3g sugar, 8g protein

TOFU-BASIL LASAGNA

WHAT'S LASAGNA WITHOUT RICOTTA, MOZZARELLA, AND PARMESAN? TO AN ITALIAN, IT'S A TRAVESTY. TO A VEGAN OR SOMEONE WITH FOOD ALLERGIES, IT'S A DELICIOUS, HEALTHY, ONE-DISH MEAL THAT'S BOUND TO ALSO PLEASE THE MEAT AND DAIRY-LOVERS AMONG US. THIS LASAGNA IN PARTICULAR HAS LITTLE DETAILS THAT MAKE IT SPECIAL: LOTS OF VEGETABLES, CREAMY TOFU FLAVORED WITH BASIL AND LEMON JUICE, AND TOASTY PINE NUTS.

Serves 10–12

TOFU-BASIL RICOTTA

1 (16-ounce) package firm tofu, well drained
2 tablespoons fresh lemon juice
½ cup reduced-fat Vegenaise
2 cloves garlic, pressed
2 tablespoons onion powder
1 teaspoon salt
2 tablespoons nutritional yeast flakes
½ cup fresh basil, finely chopped
⅛ teaspoon cayenne pepper
1 cup vegan ricotta cheese (optional)

LASAGNA

2 (16-ounce) jars vegetarian spaghetti sauce
1 (9-ounce) package egg-less lasagna noodles, cooked or no-bake
2 small zucchini, sliced
1 bunch fresh basil, loosely chopped
2 cups baby spinach
½ cup sliced mushrooms (optional)
⅓ cup pine nuts, toasted (optional)
Vegan cheese shreds, such as Daiya Mozzarella Style Cheese Shreds,
for topping (optional)

MAKE THE TOFU-BASIL RICOTTA: Remove as much moisture from the tofu as possible with a paper towel. In a large bowl, mash the tofu until it reaches a creamy, ricotta-like consistency. Combine the rest of the ingredients and mix well.

ASSEMBLE THE LASAGNA IN A 9X13 PAN AS FOLLOWS:

- 1 cup spaghetti sauce
- Lasagna noodles
- ½ of the tofu-basil ricotta, then pat down
- 1 cup spaghetti sauce
- Lasagna noodles
- Layer another 1 cup spaghetti sauce
- Vegetables: mushrooms, zucchini, most of the basil, and spinach
- Lasagna noodles
- 1 cup spaghetti sauce
- Remaining tofu-basil ricotta, then pat down
- Toasted pine nuts
- Remaining basil (optional; reserve some for serving)
- Lasagna noodles
- 1 cup spaghetti sauce
- Top with cheese (optional)

Cover with foil and bake until bubbly at 375°F, about 50 minutes. Uncover and bake for an additional 10 minutes. Remove the lasagna from the oven and let it cool for a few minutes before cutting into it. Sprinkle with additional basil just before serving.

MAKE-AHEAD TIP: Make a double batch and don't bake one of the batches. Freeze it for later, and when you want a hassle-free dinner, simply defrost it and bake as usual!

Per 1-cup serving: 225 calories, 9g fat (1g saturated fat), 0mg cholesterol, 605mg sodium, 26g carbs, 3.5g dietary fiber, 2g sugar, 8g protein

VEGETABLE POT PIE

THIS POT PIE IS A FAVORITE RECIPE HANDED DOWN TO ME FROM MY MOTHER. IT'S THE PERFECT DISH IF WHATEVER YOU'RE CRAVING IS COVERED WITH A FLAKY CRUST AND STUDDED WITH WARM, HEARTY VEGETABLES. FEEL FREE TO ADD IN SOME DICED FIRM TOFU IF YOU'D LIKE MORE PROTEIN.

Serves 6–8

CRUST:

⅓ cup boiling water
⅔ cup canola oil
2¼ cup flour (½ whole-wheat flour, ½ white flour)
1 teaspoon salt

FILLING:

⅓ cup non-hydrogenated margarine
⅓ cup whole-wheat flour
1 clove garlic, minced
1 teaspoon salt
1½ cups water
⅔ cup unsweetened soy milk
2 teaspoons McKay's Chicken Style Instant Broth and Seasoning (or other chicken-like seasoning)
celery salt, to taste
2 cups fresh or frozen mixed vegetables, diced

MAKE THE CRUST: In a medium-size bowl, mix flour and salt. In a separate bowl, pour in oil and add the boiling water while whisking vigorously. Pour the wet mixture into the dry mixture and quickly stir together. Divide dough in half and shape into balls. Between two sheets of waxed paper, roll out one ball of dough until it is large enough to fit one pie plate. Roll out the other ball of dough until it is large enough to place on top of the pie. Make sure to roll this dough out quickly, while it is still warm.

MAKE THE FILLING: In a pot over high heat, cook the vegetables in boiling water until they're barely tender, then drain. While the vegetables are cooking, prepare the sauce. In a saucepan, melt the margarine and stir in the flour, garlic, and salt. Once combined, stir in water, milk, and chicken seasoning and bring to a boil, stirring for 2 minutes. Remove from heat and combine with the cooked vegetables.

ASSEMBLE THE PIE: Preheat the oven to 425°F. Transfer the vegetable filling into a pie pan and carefully cover with the top crust. Pinch the crust to seal the edges and cut away the excess dough. Use a fork to make several small holes to allow steam to escape. Place in the oven and bake for 30-35 minutes.

Crust, per serving: 274 calories, 18.5g fat (1.4g saturated fat), 0mg cholesterol, 292mg sodium, 23.9g carbs, 0.8g dietary fiber, 3.2g protein

Filling, per serving: 128 calories, 8.1g fat (1.3g saturated fat), 0mg cholesterol, 412mg sodium, 11.5g carbs, 2.3g dietary fiber, 2.2g sugar, 2.6g protein

LENTIL ROAST

THIS ROAST MADE WITH LENTILS, NUTS, AND CORNFLAKES IS AN EXTREMELY CHEAP AND EASY WAY TO SATISFY A WHOLE FAMILY. TRY SMOTHERING IT WITH OUR **BRAZIL NUT GRAVY** (P. 275) AND SERVING IT WITH A SIDE OF ROASTED VEGETABLES FOR A HEARTY DINNER.

Serves 8–10

2 cups cooked green or brown lentils
1 cup pecans, chopped
3 cups cornflakes
2 cups unsweetened soy milk
1 medium onion, finely chopped
1 teaspoon dried sage
½ teaspoon garlic powder
1 teaspoon salt

Preheat oven to 350°F. Crush cornflakes in a plastic bag and combine all ingredients in a bowl. Continue mixing until it reaches a thick consistency, adding more cornflakes if there is any excess liquid. Then transfer the mixture to a casserole dish, and bake for 1 hour. Set aside for 10-15 minutes to let it cool, then slice into 10 portions to serve.

Per slice: 183 calories, 9g fat (1g saturated fat), 0mg cholesterol, 314mg sodium, 20g carbs, 5g dietary fiber, 2.6g sugar, 7g protein

SLOW COOKER SWEET POTATO TACOS

SLOW COOKERS ARE MAKING A COMEBACK, AND THEY'RE FINALLY GETTING THE RECOGNITION THEY DESERVE FOR BEING ABLE TO MAKE MORE THAN A BIG POT OF CHILI. FOR EXAMPLE, WHO KNEW YOU COULD MAKE TACOS IN A CROCKPOT?

Makes 10

10 corn tortillas
1 (15-ounce) can black beans, drained and rinsed
2 large sweet potatoes, diced in 1-inch cubes (about 3 cups)
¼ cup vegetable broth (low-sodium preferred)
2 tablespoons fresh lime juice
1 teaspoon ground cumin
½ teaspoon ground coriander
2 teaspoons garlic, minced
1-2 teaspoons salt, or to taste
pinch of cayenne (optional)

Spray a slow cooker with olive oil or nonstick spray. Put all the ingredients (beans, sweet potatoes, vegetable stock, lime juice, ground cumin, ground coriander, minced garlic) in the slow cooker and cook on high for about 3 hours, or until sweet potatoes are softened to your liking. Season to taste with salt and optional cayenne pepper.

Assemble the tacos. Put a generous amount of filling inside a warmed tortilla. Top with avocado, a squeeze of lime juice, and salsa.

Per taco: 151 calories, 1.2g fat (0g saturated fat), 0mg cholesterol, 275mg sodium, 31g carbs, 6g dietary fiber, 0.3g sugar, 5.4g protein

MAC & CHEEZE

MANY FOLKS DRAWN TO MAKING VEGAN DISHES MIGHT ALREADY KNOW SOME OF THE TRICKS TO MAKING A GREAT DAIRY-FREE MAC & CHEESE, BUT IF YOU HAVEN'T HEARD THEM YET: NUTRITIONAL YEAST IS KEY, SOY MILK AND TOFU ADD A DECADENT, SILKY BITE, AND MUSTARD, ALTHOUGH OPTIONAL IN THIS RECIPE, IS A BIG, BIG FLAVOR-BOOSTER.

Serves 6–8

13.25-ounce box of whole-wheat pasta, preferably macaroni

"CHEESE" SAUCE:

¾ cup unsweetened soy milk
¾ cup nutritional yeast flakes
½ cup canola or vegetable oil
½ cup water
2 tablespoons low-sodium soy sauce
¼ (16-ounce) package firm tofu
½ tablespoon garlic powder
½ tablespoon paprika
½ tablespoon salt
½ tablespoon mustard (optional)
¼ cup breadcrumbs (optional)

Cook the pasta according to package directions. While the pasta is cooking, prepare the cheese sauce by simply adding the rest of the ingredients—except the breadcrumbs—to a high-speed blender and blending until smooth. Combine the sauce with the cooked pasta and either serve immediately or cook further in the oven with the following instructions:

Preheat oven to 350°F. Add the pasta and sauce to a 9x13 casserole dish. Liberally spread breadcrumbs over the top of the dish and bake in the oven until the breadcrumbs are toasty and browned, about 10-15 minutes.

Per ¾-cup serving: 348 calories, 16g fat (1.3g saturated fat), 0mg cholesterol, 675mg sodium, 41g carbs, 5g dietary fiber, 1g sugar, 14g protein

PASTA PRIMAVERA

EVERYONE NEEDS A SIGNATURE PASTA RECIPE IN THEIR BACK POCKET. THIS MULTICOLORED, VEGETABLE-FULL DISH MIGHT BE IT. WHEN YOU HAVE A LEFTOVER FRIDGE FULL OF VEGGIES YOU DON'T KNOW WHAT TO DO WITH, STEAM THEM AND COMBINE WITH OUR THICK, CREAMY CASHEW SAUCE AND WHOLE-GRAIN PASTA FOR A WONDERFUL PRIMAVERA.

Serves 4–5

2 cups uncooked whole-wheat pasta
4 cups mixed vegetables, lightly steamed
1 recipe **Basic Cream Sauce** (p. 268)

Boil and drain pasta according to package directions. While the pasta is cooking, prepare the cream sauce and steamed vegetables. Steam the vegetables in a small amount of water, salt to taste, and set aside. Combine the cream sauce with the cooked pasta and steamed vegetables. Serve immediately.

TIP: Stir ¼ teaspoon ground nutmeg into the cream sauce to give it a more alfredo-like flavor.

PRIMAVERA CASSEROLE VARIATION: Place the pasta in a casserole dish and sprinkle with breadcrumbs. Bake the casserole the oven at 350°F until the breadcrumbs brown, and serve.

Per 1-cup serving: 305 calories, 7.5g fat (0.5g saturated fat), 0mg cholesterol, 481mg sodium, 52g carbs, 8g dietary fiber, 4.6g sugar, 10g protein

FRESH TOMATO-BASIL FOCACCIA

THIS RECIPE FOR FLAT, TUSCAN-STYLE FOCACCIA EMBEDS A VARIETY OF HERBS AND THIN SLICES OF GARLIC IN THE DOUGH BEFORE BAKING. IT'S THE PERFECT BASE FOR A HEAPING PILE OF FRESH INGREDIENTS LIKE CHERRY TOMATOES AND TORN BASIL.

Serves 2–4

1 package whole-wheat store-bought pizza dough (or homemade pizza dough)
¼ teaspoon garlic powder
½ teaspoon dried oregano
½ teaspoon dried basil
½ teaspoon dried thyme
pinch of salt
1 tablespoon extra-virgin olive oil (optional)
2 cloves garlic, sliced thinly
10-12 cherry tomatoes, halved
6-7 fresh basil leaves, roughly chopped

Preheat oven to 500°F. Place the dough in a large bowl and add the seasonings (garlic powder, dried oregano, dried basil, and dried thyme) and salt. Knead until the seasonings and salt are well incorporated.

Roll the dough out onto a floured surface. Use your fingers to lightly press the garlic slices into the top surface of the dough. Bake the focaccia until the dough is puffed, blistered, and browned, about 8-10 minutes.

Remove the focaccia from the oven and lightly brush it with olive oil (optional). Top it with the tomato halves, chopped basil, and a pinch of salt to taste.

SERVING TIP: If you're looking for a heartier meal, spread some **Pistachio-Basil Spread** (p. 260) on the focaccia before adding the tomatoes and basil, or, make the **Zesty Tomato-Basil Bruschetta** (p. 222) and spread the bruschetta on the focaccia.

Per 2-slice serving: 272 calories, 3g fat (0g saturated fat), 0mg cholesterol, 39mg sodium, 63g carbs, 7g dietary fiber, 1.2g sugar, 7g protein

KENYAN BEANS & RICE

IN KENYA, THIS DISH WOULD BE CALLED *MAHRAGWE* (SIMPLY "BEANS" IN KISWAHILI). IT'S AN EXTREMELY SIMPLE STEW OF KIDNEY BEANS, COCONUT MILK, TOMATOES, AND CURRY SPICES. IT'S EASY TO MAKE AND TASTY—AND BEST OF ALL, YOU'LL PROBABLY HAVE EVERYTHING YOU NEED IN YOUR PANTRY.

Serves 6–8

4 cups brown basmati rice, cooked
1 teaspoon extra-virgin olive oil
1 clove garlic, minced
1 small onion, chopped
2-3 teaspoons curry powder
1 (28-ounce) can diced tomatoes, juice reserved
2 (15-ounce) cans kidney beans, drained
1 (13½-ounce) can coconut milk (or light coconut milk)
salt, to taste

Cook the basmati rice according to package instructions.

In a pot over medium heat, sauté garlic and onions in oil. Add 2 teaspoons curry powder and stir. Add tomatoes with juice and simmer for about 10 minutes. Add the coconut milk and simmer for 10 minutes. Taste the mixture and add more curry powder to your liking. Add the drained beans. Cover and simmer for 15-20 minutes. Salt to taste, then serve over rice.

*Per 1 cup of sauce (with **regular** coconut milk): 291 calories, 14g fat (10g saturated fat), 0mg cholesterol, 652mg sodium, 31g carbs, 9g dietary fiber, 4g sugar, 11g protein*

*Per 1 cup of sauce (with **light** coconut milk): 180 calories, 3g fat (0.6g saturated fat), 0mg cholesterol, 635mg sodium, 28g carbs, 9g dietary fiber, 3g sugar, 11g protein*

SICILIAN TOMATO-LENTIL PASTA

LOVINGLY KNOWN AS *PASTA E LENTICCHIE* (PASTA AND LENTILS) IN CAMPANIA, ITALY, THE COMBINATION OF HUMBLE INGREDIENTS CREATE A DISH THAT SOMEHOW FEELS FAMILIAR WITH YOUR FIRST BITE.

Serves 4

½ pound whole-wheat pasta, uncooked
5 cups water
¾ cup uncooked brown lentils
2 large cloves garlic, crushed
3 tablespoons extra-virgin olive oil
1 cup canned plum tomatoes, diced and some liquid reserved
1 teaspoon salt
¼ teaspoon crushed red pepper flakes
2 tablespoons parsley, minced

In a medium saucepan, bring 5 cups of water to a boil, then add the lentils. Cook the lentils, covered, over medium-high heat until they're nearly but not entirely tender, about 20 minutes. Meanwhile, bring a separate pot of water to a boil and cook the pasta al dente.

When the lentils are nearly cooked and have absorbed all the water, add the garlic, olive oil, tomatoes, salt, and red pepper flakes. Reduce the heat to medium-low, cover, and continue to simmer briskly for another 10 minutes or until the lentils are fully tender. Add the cooked pasta and parsley to the lentils and stir everything to combine.

Add additional red pepper flakes (optional) and serve.

Per 1-cup serving: 438 calories, 11.75g fat (1.7g saturated fat), 0mg cholesterol, 728mg sodium, 68g carbs, 10g dietary fiber, 3.25g sugar, 19g protein

CREAMY MUSHROOM STROGANOFF

MANY RUSSIAN, EAST EUROPEAN, AND GERMAN DISHES ARE MEAT AND CREAM HEAVY, AND THUS RATHER DIFFICULT TO MAKE VEGAN. BUT USING CASHEWS AND MULTIPLE VARIETIES OF MUSHROOMS, THIS RECIPE REPLICATES ALL THE COMFORT AND HEARTINESS OF THE FOODS YOU LOVE.

Serves 4–6

8 cups whole-wheat pasta, uncooked
⅓ cup raw cashews
¼ (16-ounce) package silken tofu
1½ cups water, divided
1 tablespoon Bragg Liquid Aminos (or low-sodium soy sauce)
1 tablespoon McKay's Beef Style Instant Broth and Seasoning (or other beef-like seasoning)
1 tablespoon onion powder
1½ tablespoons nutritional yeast flakes
½ medium onion, julienned
1 cup fresh cremini mushrooms, sliced
1 cup fresh shiitake mushrooms, chopped

Boil and drain pasta according to package directions. While the pasta is cooking, prepare the tofu sauce base. Place the cashews and tofu in a blender with ½ cup water and blend until smooth, adding in the seasonings (Bragg Liquid Aminos, McKay's seasoning, onion powder, and nutritional yeast flakes). When the mixture is smooth, add the remaining cup of water and blend again. Set aside.

In a pan over medium heat, sauté the onions and mushrooms in a small amount of water until tender. Stir in the blended tofu sauce. Warm the mixture, making sure not to boil it, as the mixture will curdle slightly. Serve over the cooked pasta.

Per ½ cup of sauce: 72 calories, 3g fat (0.3g saturated fat), 0mg cholesterol, 336mg sodium, 8g carbs, 2g dietary fiber, 1.5g sugar, 4g protein

MUJADDARA (LEBANESE LENTILS)

AN ARTICLE BY NPR CALLED "IN PRAISE OF THE HUMBLE LENTIL" PUTS IT BEST: "I SAT BY THE WINDOW, WATCHING THE RAIN TRICKLE DOWN THE PLATE GLASS, AND SLOWLY ATE WHAT I COULDN'T PRONOUNCE: THE RICE, THE LENTILS, THE CARAMELIZED ONIONS. AT THE TIME, IT SEEMED LIKE THE BEST FOOD IN THE WORLD—FILLING, NUTTY AND EARTHEN, THE ONIONS SWEET AND CRISP ON THE EDGES. AS I WALKED THE BLOCK HOME, I MUTTERED, "*MUHDAAHRDERER, MOOJARDARAH, MURDARJERER*," STUMBLING OVER THE ROLLED "R" IN THE MIDDLE AND WONDERING HOW I WOULD GO ABOUT ORDERING IT THE NEXT TIME."

EVEN IF YOU NEVER FIGURE OUT HOW TO PROPERLY PRONOUNCE IT, HERE'S HOW YOU CAN MAKE IT WITHIN THE JUDGMENT-LESS EYES OF YOUR HOME:

Serves 6

LENTILS & RICE:

1 tablespoon extra-virgin olive oil
1 cup onion, diced
½ cup brown rice, uncooked
1 cup brown lentils, uncooked and rinsed
1 teaspoon salt
pinch of cayenne pepper

CARAMELIZED ONIONS:

1 tablespoon extra-virgin olive oil
3 large onions, julienned
pinch of salt

PREPARE THE LENTILS AND RICE: In a large, heavy bottomed pot, sauté 1 cup of diced onions in olive oil until they're slightly browned. Add both lentils and rice to the onions and sauté a few minutes longer. Add the water, salt, and cayenne pepper to the pot, then cover the pot and simmer over low heat for about 1½ hours. Stir the mixture from time to time and add water as needed. Prepare the caramelized onions while the lentils and rice simmer.

In a separate pan, prepare the onions. Heat the olive oil to medium-high temperature in a large pan. Add the onions and salt to the pan, stirring constantly until they're translucent and very soft, nearly melting consistency—it may take up to 30 minutes. If the onions stick to the bottom of the pan, add a very small amount of water and stir vigorously.

TO SERVE: Top the lentils and rice with the onions and serve hot, at room temperature, or cold.

Per ¾-cup serving: 192 calories, 5.2g fat (0.7g saturated fat), 0mg cholesterol, 415mg sodium, 21g carbs, 4g dietary fiber, 0g sugar, 4.3g protein

ASIAN SHIITAKE, KALE & RICE BOWL

KALE IS A MEMBER OF THE CANCER-FIGHTING CRUCIFEROUS FAMILY OF VEGETABLES AND IS PACKED FULL OF FIBER AND ANTIOXIDANTS. THAT, IN COMBINATION WITH COMMON ASIAN INGREDIENTS LIKE SOY SAUCE, WASABI PASTE, RED PEPPER FLAKES, AND SHIITAKE MUSHROOMS, MAKES FOR A BALANCED AND UNIQUE LUNCH OR DINNER IN A BOWL.

Serves 4–6

4 cups cooked brown rice
2 teaspoons extra-virgin olive oil
1 small onion, chopped
2 cloves garlic, minced
2 tablespoons low-sodium soy sauce
1 tablespoon sesame seeds
½ teaspoon wasabi paste (optional)
½ teaspoon red pepper flakes
1 cup shiitake mushrooms, sliced
½ (16-ounce) package firm tofu, drained and cubed
⅓ cup water
4 cups packed kale, ribs removed and chopped (about 1 bunch)

Cook the rice according to package directions.

While the rice is cooking, prepare the rest of the ingredients by first heating olive oil in a deep pan or wok. Add the onion and garlic and sauté for 3 minutes. Add the soy sauce, sesame seeds, wasabi paste, red pepper flakes, mushrooms, and tofu and stir well. Sauté for an additional 5 minutes. Then, stir in ⅓ cup water and the kale and sauté until the kale is slightly wilted and crisp-tender, about 4 minutes.

Portion the rice into 2-4 bowls and top with the kale mixture.

Per ¾ cup (without rice): 163 calories, 7g fat (1g saturated fat), 0mg cholesterol, 493mg sodium, 18g carbs, 5g dietary fiber, 4g sugar, 11g protein

QUICK PERSONAL PIZZA

THIS IS MORE A GUIDELINE THAN A RECIPE, BUT IT'S WHAT I USE WHEN THE FAMILY IS HANKERING FOR HOMEMADE PIZZA BUT NOTHING AND THERE'S A FEW PANTRY AND FRIDGE STAPLES TO MAKE IT HAPPEN.

CRUST: whole-grain pita bread, hamburger buns, naan, lavash, baguette, flatbread, English muffins

SAUCE/BASE: **Simple Basil Pesto** (p. 259), **Basic Cream Sauce** (p. 268), fresh tomatoes simmered down with fresh herbs, or a whole head of roasted garlic smeared onto the crust with some olive oil

CHEESE SUBSTITUTE (OPTIONAL): Daiya cheese, especially Daiya Mozzarella Style Shreds, is a wonderful cheese substitute and melts down like real cheese

ENDLESS TOPPINGS: fresh tomatoes, bell peppers, mushrooms, olives, red onions, green onions, artichoke hearts, fresh basil, zucchini, pesto, sun dried tomatoes, jalapeño peppers, roasted garlic, asparagus, spinach, etc.

Preheat oven to 375°F. Spread base sauce on the bread, then add the cheese and other toppings.

Bake in the oven on a baking sheet or a pizza stone until the toppings and cheese are bubbly and the crust's edges are toasty and crisp, about 12-15 minutes. Sprinkle a pinch of basil, oregano, or crushed red pepper on top and serve.

Per serving (based on 1 whole-wheat pita bread + ¼ cup marinara sauce + ¼ cup Daiya Mozzarella Style Shreds): 284 calories, 9.5g fat (2.5g saturated fat), 0mg cholesterol, 788mg sodium, 41.7g carbs, 6.9g dietary fiber, 3g sugar, 7.9g protein)

HOMEMADE NACHOS

ANYTIME OF THE YEAR IS A GOOD TIME FOR NACHOS, ESPECIALLY IF YOU'RE ENTERTAINING A BIG, BOISTEROUS GROUP OF FRIENDS. THIS RECIPE IS QUICK, EASY TO ADJUST TO YOUR PERSONAL PREFERENCES, AND EVERYBODY SEEMS TO LOVE THEM. WHEN YOU'RE TRYING TO BE VEGAN OR ENTERTAIN VEGAN FRIENDS, NACHOS MAY SEEM OUT OF THE QUESTION, BUT THIS RECIPE ANSWERS THAT QUESTION WITH A RESOUNDING "*YES*"!

Serves 4–6

4 cups corn tortilla chips

½ cup **Nacho Cheese-Style Sauce** (p. 270), optional
¼ cup Tofutti sour cream, optional
1 (15-ounce) can vegetarian refried beans, warmed
⅓ cup salsa of choice
¼ cup black olives
¼ cup lettuce, chopped
1 avocado, diced
Additional vegetables, such as bell peppers, zucchini, mushrooms, optional

Make the **Nacho Cheese-Style Sauce**.

Preheat the oven to 350°F. Place the tortilla chips on a large cooking sheet or an oven safe plate. Cover the chips with beans, Nacho Cheese-Style Sauce, salsa, olives, and any additional vegetables (bell peppers, zucchini, mushrooms).

Bake the nachos until the chips are crispy and the cheese is bubbling, it shouldn't take much longer than a few minutes. Top with the lettuce and avocado, then serve.

Per 1-cup serving: 378 calories, 18g fat (3g saturated fat), 0mg cholesterol, 1006mg sodium, 38g carbs. 10g dietary fiber, 2.5g sugar, 10g protein

THE VEGGIE BURGER

Veggie burger. To many, the expression itself is a contradiction in terms. If you've never had a veggie burger, the whole notion of making a grilled patty without meat may seem kind of crazy. If you're one of the many people who have experienced a lousy veggie burger, then you might not wish to repeat the experience anytime soon. But let me tell you, all it takes is the right recipe (and some practice).

WHAT IS A VEGGIE BURGER ANYWAY? Until recently, most veggie burgers were heavily processed and manufactured to resemble beef: color, smell, and even little artificial grill marks. They may have satisfied the new vegetarian who really missed meat, but they leave something to be desired for those who are interested in delicious, plant-based cuisine. All of that changes with whole-food veggie burgers—creative combinations of grains, legumes, nuts, and seeds.

What I love most about veggie burgers is their versatility. Sure, you can place them between a whole grain bun, slather them with ketchup, and eat them traditionally. But you can also serve them atop a giant salad, stuff them into a pita with lettuce and tomato, wrap them into romaine or butter lettuce leaves for a lighter spin on a "wrap," place them between sandwich bread if buns aren't to be found, or even chop them into a leftover rice dish. There's really no limit on what to do with them.

OAT BURGER

Makes 6–8

3 cups water
¼ cup Bragg Liquid Aminos
1 tablespoon McKay's Beef Style Instant Broth and Seasoning (or other beef-like seasoning)
1 teaspoon Italian seasoning
1 teaspoon garlic powder
½ tablespoon onion powder
½ teaspoon salt
3 tablespoons nutritional yeast flakes
¼ cup dry onion flakes (or 1 finely diced onion)
3 cups quick oats
½ cup walnuts or pecans, ground

Preheat oven to 375°F. Place all ingredients except the oats and nuts in a high-speed blender. Cover and turn the blender on for 2-3 seconds, just enough for the ingredients to run through the blades and get chopped finely but not pureed.

Place the mixture in a saucepan and simmer everything together for 3 minutes, then remove from the heat and stir in the quick oats and nuts. Allow it to cool.

Using an ice cream scoop or your hands, shape the mixture into 6-8 balls, placing them on a nonstick baking sheet. Press down with the palm of your hand to make each patty ¼-inch thick and place them in the oven. Bake for 25-30 minutes, flipping them after 15 minutes so that both sides are golden brown.

VARIATION 1: Try adding a tablespoon of molasses and a tablespoon of tomato puree for a richer flavor.

VARIATION 2: Make a chili-oat burger by replacing the Italian seasoning with 1 teaspoon cumin, and the McKay's Beef Style Seasoning with 1 tablespoon chili powder.

Per patty: 172 calories, 6g fat (0.7g saturated fat), 0g cholesterol, 545mg sodium, 26g carbs, 26g carbs, 1.5g sugar, 6.5g protein

SOUTHWEST BLACK BEAN BURGER

Makes 4

½ yellow onion, chopped
½ jalapeño, seeded and chopped
3 garlic cloves
1 (15-ounce) can black beans, drained
½ cup + 2 tablespoons rolled oats
½ cup frozen corn
1 tablespoon fresh cilantro, minced
2 teaspoons ground cumin
½ teaspoon curry powder
¼ teaspoon cayenne pepper
¼ cup breadcrumbs
½ teaspoon salt, or more to taste

Place the onion, jalapeño, and garlic in a food processor and pulse 5-6 times. Add the beans, oats, corn, cilantro, cumin, curry powder, and cayenne, season to taste with salt, and pulse 8 times. Scrape down the sides of the food processor and pulse an additional 5-8 times, depending on your desired texture.

Drizzle a teaspoon of oil into a skillet and heat to medium. Form the burger mixture into 4 equal patties. Cook the patties for 5-7 minutes on each side, or until a crust develops and the patties are heated through.

Remove the patties from the heat and place onto burger buns. Assemble the burger with toppings and condiments of your choice.

Per patty: 133 calories, 2g fat (0g saturated fat), 0mg cholesterol, 347mg sodium, 25g carbs, 6g dietary fiber, 2g sugar, 6g protein

BAKED FALAFEL

ONE BITE INTO A WARM WHOLE-WHEAT PITA STUFFED WITH FRESHLY BAKED FALAFEL, TOMATOES, AND CUCUMBERS, AND YOU'LL NEVER THINK ABOUT ORDERING DEEP-FRIED, TAKEOUT FALAFEL AGAIN.

Makes 30

1½ (15-ounce) cans chickpeas, drained and ¼ cup liquid reserved
¼ cup fresh lemon juice
¼ cup sesame seeds (optional)
¼ cup fresh cilantro or flat-leaf parsley, chopped (or 2 tablespoons dried)
½ teaspoon dried basil
¼ teaspoon dried oregano
1 teaspoon cumin
¼ teaspoon cayenne
½ teaspoon paprika
1 teaspoon salt
1 small onion, finely chopped
1-2 cloves garlic
1-1½ cups breadcrumbs

Preheat the oven to 350°F. In a food processor, add the chickpeas, fresh lemon juice, onion, garlic, and parsley (if using fresh), and puree until smooth. Put the bean mixture in a large bowl and add all other dry seasonings (oregano, basil, cumin, cayenne, paprika, and salt). Then, stir in the breadcrumbs to hold the mixture together. Add more breadcrumbs if the mixture isn't holding together.

Roll into 1-inch balls and place them on a cookie sheet. Lightly spray the falafel with oil and bake in the oven for 10-15 minutes per side or until the falafel are lightly browned. Test for doneness by pressing the outside with your finger. The falafel should be moist inside and give to the pressure of your finger.

Per 3-falafel serving: 138 calories, 1.5g fat (0.2g saturated fat), 0mg cholesterol, 994mg sodium, 27g carbs, 4g dietary fiber, 5.3g protein

TOFU SALADS

THESE TOFU EGGLESS SALADS ARE SURPRISINGLY CONVINCING AND, DARE I SAY, EVEN BETTER THAN THE ORIGINAL.

SIMPLE TOFU SALAD

Serves 4–6

1 (16-ounce) package firm tofu, drained
½ cup reduced-fat Vegenaise
¼ cup sweet pickle relish
4 teaspoons Dijon mustard
4 teaspoons lemon juice
¼ cup red onion, finely diced
½ cup celery, finely diced
1 tablespoon carrot, grated (optional)
¼ teaspoon turmeric
salt to taste

Using a paper towel or dishtowel, squeeze as much moisture from the tofu as possible. In a medium bowl, use your hands to crumble the tofu. Mix the crumbled tofu with the rest of the ingredients. Serve between slices of whole-wheat bread or crumble on top of salad.

Per ¾-cup serving: 135 calories, 11g fat (0.6g saturated fat), 0mg cholesterol, 327mg sodium, 6g carbs, 1g dietary fiber, 2g sugar, 5.6g protein

CURRIED TOFU SALAD

Serves 4–6

1 (16-ounce) package firm tofu, drained
¼ cup celery, finely diced
1 tablespoon green onion, minced
½ teaspoon turmeric
¼ teaspoon curry powder
¼ teaspoon ground cumin
¼ teaspoon ground coriander
2 teaspoons nutritional yeast flakes
½ teaspoon salt
3 tablespoons reduced-fat Vegenaise

Using a paper towel or dishtowel, squeeze as much moisture out of the tofu as possible. In a medium-sized bowl, use your hands to crumble the tofu. Mix the crumbled tofu with the rest of the ingredients. Serve between slices of whole-wheat bread or crumble on top of salad.

Per ¾-cup serving: 98 calories, 7g fat (0.7g saturated fat), 0mg cholesterol, 375mg sodium, 3.2g carbs, 1.3g dietary fiber, 0.5g sugar, 7.4g protein

MOCK TUNA SALAD

COMING FROM A PALATE THAT HAS TASTED REAL TUNA SALAD BEFORE, BELIEVE ME: THIS TASTES LIKE THE REAL THING, INCREDIBLY AND ALMOST EERILY SO. SERVE IT AS YOU WOULD OTHER TUNA SALAD: ON CRACKERS, BETWEEN WHOLE-GRAIN BREAD SLICES, IN A WRAP, OR WITH CELERY STICKS.

Serves 4–6

1 (15-ounce) can of chickpeas, drained
¼ cup reduced-fat Vegenaise
⅓ cup celery, finely chopped
2 tablespoons sweet onion, finely chopped
½ tablespoon nutritional yeast flakes
1 green onion, chopped
1 teaspoon low-sodium soy sauce

In a medium bowl, mash the chickpeas with a fork and combine with the rest of the ingredients. Serve on whole-wheat bread with lettuce.

Per ¾-cup serving: 128 calories, 5g fat (0.1g saturated fat), 0mg cholesterol, 354mg sodium, 18g carbs, 3.5g dietary fiber, 0g sugar, 4g protein

BEAN & GREEN CHILE QUESADILLAS

QUESADILLAS, ANOTHER RECIPE YOU MIGHT HAVE THOUGHT WOULD BECOME OBSOLETE IN YOUR PLANT-BASED REPERTOIRE. FEEL FREE TO KICK THIS RECIPE UP A NOTCH WITH SOME SPINACH, MUSHROOMS, AND ONIONS FOR A BALANCED LUNCH.

Serves 4–6

6 whole-wheat flour tortillas
1 teaspoon extra-virgin olive oil
1 clove garlic, minced
1 (6-ounce) can diced fire-roasted green chiles
1 (15-ounce) can refried beans (Rosarita's Fat-Free Zesty Refried Beans preferred)
1/2 cup Daiya Cheddar Style Cheese Shreds
Tofutti sour cream, salsa, or guacamole, to serve

Heat oil in a medium pan and add the minced garlic, green chiles, and refried beans. Cook over medium heat for 5 minutes, continuously stirring to prevent the beans from burning. Turn off heat and stir in Daiya cheese. The cheese does not need to melt.

Lay down a tortilla in a separate skillet and evenly spread with a layer of filling. Place a second tortilla on top and use a spatula to flatten the tortillas together. Cook over medium-high heat on both sides until the edges are crisp and golden brown. Cut into wedges and serve with Tofutti sour cream, salsa, or guacamole.

Per quesadilla: 251 calories, 6.2g fat (1.1g saturated fat), 0mg cholesterol, 586mg sodium, 39.6g carbs, 8.5g dietary fiber, 1.9g sugar, 8.6g protein

HUMMUS WRAP

BALANCED, SIMPLE, DELICIOUS. TRY IT ON A SUN-DRIED TOMATO, SPINACH, OR REGULAR WHOLE-WHEAT FLOUR TORTILLA!

Makes 2 wraps

2 (12-inch) whole-grain tortillas
½ cup **Hummus** (p. 256)
1 packed cup spinach or kale
½ cup tomato, diced
½ avocado, sliced
½ cucumber, sliced

Microwave the tortilla for a few seconds to make it pliable. Spread the hummus over the tortilla, then layer on the assorted vegetables. Wrap the tortilla like a burrito and enjoy.

Per wrap: 380 calories, 24g fat (4g saturated fat), 0mg cholesterol, 381mg sodium, 36g carbs, 8g dietary fiber, 3g sugar, 9g protein

ALT SANDWICH

AVOCADO, LETTUCE, TOMATO. THE BLT, AN AMERICAN LUNCHTIME CLASSIC, GETS A TWIST WITH LUXURIOUSLY CREAMY AVOCADO.

Makes 2 sandwiches

4 slices whole-grain bread
2 tablespoons **Pistachio-Basil Spread** (p. 260)
4 lettuce leaves
1 tomato, sliced
¼ avocado, sliced
salt, to taste

Spread ½ tablespoon of Pistachio-Basil Spread on each bottom bread half. Arrange avocado slices, tomato slices, and lettuce leaves on top. Close the sandwiches, cut in half, and serve.

Per sandwich: 296 calories, 13g fat (2g saturated fat), 0mg cholesterol, 304mg sodium, 35g carbs, 7g dietary fiber, 5g sugar, 12g protein

GRILLED CHEESE-STYLE SANDWICH

GOOEY CHEESE? CHECK. TOASTY BREAD? CHECK. TOMATO SOUP? CHECK (**CREAM OF TOMATO SOUP, P. 199**).

Makes 2 sandwiches

4 slices whole-grain bread
½ cup Daiya Mozzarella Style Shreds
½ cup black beans
½ tomato, sliced into 4 rounds and patted dry

Heat a pan over medium-low heat and place 2 slices of bread on the pan. Add 2 slices of bread. Add a thin layer of cheese, beans, and 2 tomato rounds to each slice. Sprinkle another layer of cheese, and cover with the remaining 2 slices. Press down firmly with a spatula. Heat until the bread is golden brown and the cheese is lightly melted, then flip over and toast the other side.

Per sandwich: 305 calories, 9g fat (2g saturated fat), 0mg cholesterol, 698mg sodium, 50g carbs, 11g dietary fiber, 4g sugar, 11g protein

Sun-Dried Tomato, Almond & Rice Salad

Black Bean, Corn & Quinoa Salad

Queen of Greens Salad

Creamy Pasta Salad

Tabbouleh

Italian Chopped Salad

Roasted Beet & Carrot Salad

Broccolini & Grape Salad

Fresh Watermelon-Mango Salad

Butter Lettuce Salad with Candied Pecans

Romaine Citrus Salad (left)

SALADS

SUN-DRIED TOMATO, ALMOND & RICE SALAD

NUTTY WILD AND BROWN RICE COMBINE WITH JUICY BURSTS OF SUN-DRIED TOMATO, CREAMY AVOCADO, AND CRUNCHY BITS OF CELERY AND ALMOND. PACK THIS INTO A PICNIC BASKET OR LUNCH PAIL FOR A BALANCED MAIN DISH OR SIDE SALAD.

Makes 2–4 main servings

2½ cups long-grain rice blend, cooked
½ cup marinated sun-dried tomatoes, coarsely chopped
1 ripe avocado, diced
1 stalk celery, finely chopped
¼ cup almond slivers
3 leaves fresh basil, julienned
1 tablespoon fresh lemon juice
1 teaspoon garlic powder
1 teaspoon salt

In a large mixing bowl, combine all ingredients and mix well.

Per 1-cup serving: 307 calories: 12.3g fat (1.6g saturated fat), 0mg cholesterol, 384mg sodium, 44g carbs, 4.8g dietary fiber, 1.8g sugar, 6.8g protein

BLACK BEAN, CORN & QUINOA SALAD

QUICK-COOKING, HIGH IN PROTEIN, EASY TO DIGEST, AND WITH A SUPERFOOD LABEL TO BOOT, IT'S NO SMALL WONDER THAT QUINOA'S (PRONOUNCED "KEEN-WAH") POPULARITY HAS SURGED IN RECENT YEARS. ALTHOUGH QUINOA IS OFTEN USED AS A REPLACEMENT FOR RICE WITH STEWS OR STIR FRIES, IT'S SOMETIMES BEST SERVED COLD, AS THE BASE FOR A FILLING, GRAIN-BASED SALAD LIKE THIS ONE. QUINOA PAIRS BEAUTIFULLY WITH OTHER PERUVIAN STAPLES LIKE CORN AND BLACK BEANS, TURNING THIS DISH INTO A PLATE OF FOOD THAT IS AS PRETTY AND COLORFUL AS IT IS DELICIOUS. IT'S A SALAD THAT KEEPS WELL IN THE FRIDGE FOR AT LEAST A FEW DAYS.

Makes 4–6 main servings

1 teaspoon extra-virgin olive oil

1 onion, chopped

3 cloves garlic, minced

¾ cup quinoa, uncooked

1½ cups vegetable broth (low-sodium preferred)

1 teaspoon ground cumin

¼ teaspoon cayenne pepper

salt to taste

1 cup frozen corn kernels

2 (15-ounce) cans black beans, rinsed and drained

½ cup fresh cilantro, chopped

1 lime, juiced (2 tablespoons)

1 jalapeño, seeded and finely diced (optional)

Over medium heat, heat oil in a saucepan and sauté the onion and garlic until they're soft and translucent. Add the quinoa to the pan and cover with vegetable broth. Season with cumin, cayenne pepper, and salt, then bring the mixture to a boil. Cover, reduce the heat and simmer for 20 minutes, stirring occasionally.

Add the frozen corn to the pan and continue to simmer for 5 more minutes. Mix in the black beans, cilantro, lime juice, and optional jalapeño and cook until the beans are heated through.

Per 1-cup serving: 329 calories, 4.8g fat (0.5g saturated fat), 0mg cholesterol, 288mg sodium, 55.2g carbs, 13g dietary fiber, 2.5g sugar, 17.5g protein

QUEEN OF GREENS SALAD

FACT: KALE IS ONE OF THE HEALTHIEST VEGETABLES ON THE PLANET. SO MUCH SO THAT IT'S BEING CALLED "THE NEW BEEF," "THE QUEEN OF GREENS," AND "A NUTRITIONAL POWERHOUSE." WHY? WELL, IT'S LOW IN CALORIES, HIGH IN FIBER, IRON, CALCIUM, AND VITAMINS K AND C, HAS 0 FAT, IS FILLED WITH POWERFUL ANTIOXIDANTS, IS A GREAT ANTI-INFLAMMATORY FOOD, AND IS GOOD FOR CARDIOVASCULAR SUPPORT. AS MUCH OF THIS COOKBOOK MIGHT SUGGEST, WE LOVE KALE AND HOPE YOU WILL TOO. HERE'S HOW YOU CAN START:

1. Wash your fresh kale greens. Run each leaf under warm to hot water and wash any grit away. Then, refresh the leaves by running them all under ice cold water.

2. Prep the kale. Remove the thick stems from the leaves and discard. Place chopped kale in a large bowl and sprinkle with a little salt and lemon juice. Using your hands, massage the leaves until the kale is reduced to half its original volume, and is no longer bitter.

3. Make your dressing in a small bowl. (See "Sauces, Dips & Dressings" for ideas.)

4. Mix the dressing with the kale, along with any additional ingredients such as veggies, fresh or dried fruits, and nuts.

5. Chill. Allow at least 20 minutes for the dressing to really sink into the ingredients. Plus, chilling everything ensures a refreshing and tasty cold salad. You could make this salad the night before you serve it, but make sure you eat the greens within 48 hours.

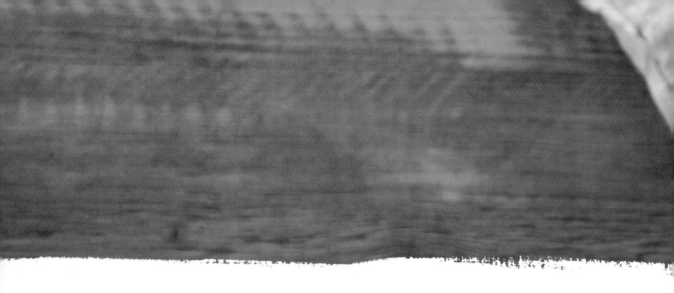

CREAMY PASTA SALAD

SOMETIMES, YOU JUST NEED THINGS TO BE EASY. YOU NEED LUNCH OR DINNER TO TAKE LESS THAN HALF AN HOUR TO PREPARE, AND YOU WANT TO MAKE IT EARLY IN THE DAY SO THAT IT'S READY WHEN YOU ARE. THIS PASTA SALAD IS FOR JUST SUCH A DAY. (IT DOESN'T HURT THAT IT'S CHEERFULLY BRIGHT AND IDEAL FOR EATING OUTSIDE IN THE SUN.) THIS PERFECT PASTA SALAD REALLY ONLY TAKES AS LONG TO MAKE AS YOUR PASTA TAKES TO COOK.

Makes 10-12 side servings

½ pound whole-wheat pasta shells

2 cups frozen white corn, thawed

6 scallions, thinly sliced

1 yellow or orange bell pepper, seeded and diced

2 cups cherry tomatoes, halved

½ cup reduced-fat Vegenaise

¼ cup Tofutti sour cream

¼ cup lemon juice (2 medium lemons)

2 teaspoons salt

¾ cup fresh dill, minced

Cook pasta according to package instructions and place in a large bowl with corn. (If using fresh corn, add the corn to the boiling pasta water about 2 minutes before the pasta is cooked, then drain with the pasta.) Then, add the scallions, diced pepper, and tomatoes, tossing gently to combine. Set aside to cool.

While the pasta is cooling, whisk together the Vegenaise, sour cream, lemon juice, and salt. Pour the mixture over the pasta and mix well to incorporate the ingredients. Stir in the dill and salt to taste.

Cover with clear wrap and chill for 4-6 hours to let the flavors marinate. Serve chilled.

Per ½-cup serving: 147 calories, 7g fat (1g saturated fat), 0mg cholesterol, 467mg sodium, 20g carbs, 3g dietary fiber, 1g sugar, 4g protein

TABBOULEH

IT'S A FOOLPROOF, CLASSIC ARABIC DISH THAT REALLY ONLY REQUIRES YOU TO COOK THE GRAIN, CHOP THE VEGETABLES, POUR ON THE LIQUIDS, AND MIX. LIKE MANY OTHER STAPLE DISHES, THIS ONE CAN BE MIXED UP AND ADAPTED TO YOUR PREFERENCES. CONSIDER USING QUINOA OR COUSCOUS INSTEAD OF BULGUR, OR ADD CHOPPED CUCUMBERS OR SUN-DRIED TOMATOES FOR A DIFFERENT FLAVOR PROFILE.

Makes 8–10 side servings

½ cup bulgur wheat
2 cups fresh parsley, minced
1 cup fresh mint, minced
2 cups tomatoes, seeded and chopped
1 small red onion, finely chopped
1 tablespoon extra-virgin olive oil
¼ cup fresh lemon juice
salt, to taste

Soak the bulgur in room-temperature water and cover until the bulgur becomes tender, about 30 minutes. Drain well, squeezing out as much water as possible.

Combine the bulgur with parsley, mint, tomatoes, and onion. Whisk the olive oil with lemon juice and toss with the salad. Season with salt to taste.

Per ½-cup serving: 97 calories, 5.7g fat (0.9g saturated fat), 0mg cholesterol, 36mg sodium, 11g carbs, 3.5g dietary fiber, 1.7g sugar, 2.4g protein

ITALIAN CHOPPED SALAD

VEGETARIAN ANTIPASTO INGREDIENTS LIKE PEPPERS AND ARTICHOKES ARE SLICED AND DICED TO MAKE THIS SUBSTANTIAL SALAD.

Serves 6–8

1 head iceberg lettuce, chopped
½ red bell pepper, chopped
½ green bell pepper, chopped
3 green onions, chopped
½ (15-ounce) can chickpeas, drained and rinsed
½ cup green olives, chopped
½ cup marinated artichokes, chopped
½ cup tomatoes, chopped
Italian dressing of choice

Combine all ingredients and serve.

Per 1-cup serving: 109 calories, 7g fat (1g saturated fat), 0mg cholesterol, 271mg sodium, 12g carbs, 4g dietary fiber, 3g sugar, 3g protein

ROASTED BEET & CARROT SALAD

THE RECIPE IS SIMPLE, BUT THE UNIQUE ROASTY FLAVOR AND SHEER BEAUTY MAKES IT THE PERFECT DISH TO BRING TO A WINTER POTLUCK DINNER.

Serves 4–6

3 small beets, peeled and thinly sliced
3 carrots, peeled and thinly sliced
salt, to taste
2 teaspoons extra-virgin olive oil
¼ cup pecans, toasted and chopped
1 tablespoon fresh tarragon, chopped (optional)

Preheat the oven to 400°F. Mix all ingredients together, except the tarragon and pecans. Layer the sliced beets and carrots on a roasting pan. Roast for 25 minutes, turning occasionally, then remove from the oven and sprinkle with pecans and tarragon before serving.

Per ½-cup serving: 97 calories, 6g fat (0.5g saturated fat), 0mg cholesterol, 225mg sodium, 11g carbs, 4g dietary fiber, 7g sugar, 2g protein

BROCCOLINI & GRAPE SALAD

BROCCOLINI IS A GREEN VEGETABLE SIMILAR TO BROCCOLI, BUT WITH SMALLER FLORETS AND LONGER THIN STALKS. BASICALLY, IT LOOKS AND TASTES LIKE A HYBRID OF BROCCOLI AND ASPARAGUS.

Serves 3–5

DRESSING:

½ teaspoon Bragg Liquid Aminos (or low-sodium soy sauce)
1 tablespoon fresh lemon juice
1 tablespoon agave nectar
½ clove garlic
¼ teaspoon salt

SALAD:

1 bundle broccolini
½ cup red grapes, halved
¼ cup dried cranberries
¼ cup almonds, toasted and chopped

PREPARE THE DRESSING: Mix all ingredients, then set aside.

Lightly steam the broccolini until it's slightly tender but still crunchy. Quickly run cold water over the broccolini to stop the cooking process. When cool, combine with the rest of the ingredients (grapes, cranberries, almonds) and the dressing.

Per ½-cup serving: 81 calories, 3g fat (0.2g saturated fat), 0mg cholesterol, 129mg sodium, 12g carbs, 2.3g dietary fiber, 9g sugar, 2g protein

FRESH WATERMELON-MANGO SALAD

FEW THINGS ARE LOVELIER OR MORE REFRESHING THAN A SALAD OF FRESHLY CUT FRUIT. THE ONLY WAY TO MAKE AN ALREADY-GREAT FRUIT SALAD BETTER? A DRIZZLE OF BRIGHT, LIGHTLY SWEETENED LIME-AGAVE DRESSING.

Serves 4–6

1 tablespoon fresh lime juice
1 tablespoon agave nectar
2 cups watermelon, cubed
1 large mango, cubed
1 cup raspberries
1 banana, sliced

In a small bowl, mix the lime juice and agave nectar until well combined. Pour over the fruit and gently toss to combine.

Per ¾-cup serving: 78 calories, 0.5g fat (0.1g saturated fat), 0mg cholesterol, 2mg sodium, 20g carbs, 3g dietary fiber, 14g sugar, 1g protein

BUTTER LETTUCE SALAD WITH CANDIED PECANS

DON'T LET THE LONG INGREDIENTS LIST SCARE YOU AWAY! THIS LOVELY SALAD IS ONE OF MY FAVORITES AND COMPLETELY WORTH THE (MINIMAL) TROUBLE. *AND* YOU CAN MAKE A BIG BATCH OF THE CANDIED PECANS AHEAD OF TIME!

Serves 4–6

SALAD:

1 head butter lettuce, gently torn
1 apple (preferably Pink Lady), unpeeled and sliced thinly
3 tablespoons currants (or dried cranberries)
¼ cup red onion, sliced thinly

CANDIED PECANS:

½ cup raw pecans
⅛ cup brown sugar
2 tablespoons water
¼ teaspoon cinnamon
small pinch cayenne pepper

DRESSING:

2 tablespoons fresh lemon juice
½ tablespoon of canola oil
2 teaspoons sugar
¼–½ teaspoon salt

MAKE THE CANDIED PECANS: Add the brown sugar, water, cinnamon, and cayenne pepper to a saucepan, then bring to a boil. Add the pecans and stir for 2 minutes. Transfer the coated pecans to a sheet of cookie sheet lined with wax paper and bake for 6 minutes at 350°F.

Whisk all dressing ingredients together to combine. Toss the dressing, candied pecans, apple slices, and lettuce together.

Per 1-cup serving: 151 calories, 9g fat (3g saturated fat), 0mg cholesterol, 101mg sodium, 19g carbs, 3g dietary fiber, 13g sugar, 1.5g protein

ROMAINE CITRUS SALAD

COUNT 'EM: 1-2-3. THREE INGREDIENTS, PLUS AN EQUALLY SIMPLE DRESSING EQUALS A QUICK SALAD THAT WORKS EVEN FOR SPECIAL OCCASIONS. CRISP, REFRESHING, AND SLIGHTLY TANGY-SWEET, THIS ONE IS A NEWFOUND FAMILY FAVORITE THAT I'M REALLY EXCITED TO SHARE WITH YOU.

Serves 8–10

1 recipe **Agave-Orange Dressing** (p. 263)
2 heads romaine lettuce, thinly chopped
1 (11-ounce) can mandarin orange segments, drained
⅓ cup almond slivers

In a large bowl, combine all of the ingredients with the Agave-Orange Dressing.

Per ¾-cup serving: 72 calories, 3g fat (0.2g saturated fat), 0mg cholesterol, 31mg sodium, 13g carbs, 2g dietary fiber, 10g sugar, 2g protein

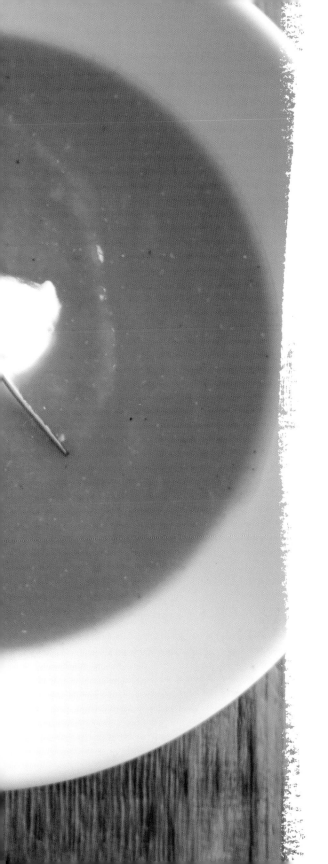

SOUPS & STEWS

THAI CURRY SOUP

THE INTERNATIONAL FOODS AISLE IS OVERWHELMING, NO? IT'S HARD ENOUGH TO READ THE LABELS OF FOODS YOU NORMALLY BUY, MUCH LESS A LIST OF INGREDIENTS YOU CAN'T PRONOUNCE. THIS THAI-INSPIRED SOUP RECIPE MEETS YOU RIGHT IN THE MIDDLE, GENTLY STEERING YOU TOWARD MORE EXOTIC FLAVORS, BUT WITH FAMILIAR INGREDIENTS THAT YOU PROBABLY ALREADY HAVE IN YOUR PANTRY.

Serves 6–8

1 teaspoon extra-virgin olive oil
1 clove garlic, pressed
1 red or orange bell pepper, chopped
¼ head cauliflower, chopped
1 cup onion, chopped
2 red potatoes, chopped into small chunks
⅓ head cabbage, chopped
1 cup green beans, diced
2 cans coconut milk
2 cups water
2 tablespoons curry powder
2 tablespoons McKay's Chicken Style Instant Broth and Seasoning (or other chicken-like seasoning)
½ teaspoon salt
2 tablespoons maple syrup (or agave nectar)
⅓ cup cilantro, chopped (optional)

Heat olive oil in a large pot over medium heat and sauté the garlic and vegetables (bell pepper, cauliflower, onion, potatoes, cabbage, and green beans).

Add the coconut milk and water, and bring to a boil. Add the remaining ingredients (curry powder, chicken seasoning, salt, maple syrup). Slightly turn down the heat and continue cooking until the vegetables are tender but not overcooked. Garnish with cilantro, if desired.

Per 1-cup serving: 262 calories, 17.5g fat (14.7g saturated fat), 0mg cholesterol, 514mg sodium, 25.9g carbs, 5.4g dietary fiber, 9.2g sugar, 4.2g protein

CREAMY POTATO SOUP

THIS IS ONE OF THE EASIEST SOUPS IN THIS COOKBOOK, AND CAN BE DRESSED UP OR DOWN IN ANY DIRECTION. I LOVE ADDING GREEN BEANS OR FRESH PEAS.

Serves 4–6

4 red potatoes, peeled and diced
5 cups water, divided
1 cup raw cashews
3 teaspoons onion powder
2 teaspoons salt
1 teaspoon fresh rosemary, thyme, or basil, minced (optional)

Combine the potatoes with 4 cups of water in a large pot over high heat and bring to a boil. Meanwhile, in a high-speed blender, blend the cashews, onion salt, and 1 cup of water until the mixture is very smooth.

When the potatoes are tender, add the cashew soup base to the pot. Heat for 5 minutes, stirring constantly to avoid burning the cream. Stir in herbs, if using, then serve.

Per 1-cup serving: 277 calories, 13g fat (2.6g saturated fat), 0mg cholesterol, 463mg sodium, 36.2g carbs, 3.8g dietary fiber, 3.1g sugar, 7.4g protein

KALE & WHITE BEAN SOUP

THINK OF THIS AS A DELICIOUS MINESTRONE SOUP, MINUS THE CARB-LADEN PASTA SHELLS. RATHER, WE FOCUS ON BUTTERY BEANS FOR PROTEIN (HEAR THAT, VEGAN NAYSAYERS?) AND THE MOST NUTRIENT-DENSE VEGGIE, KALE, FOR A HEARTY AND WELL-BALANCED WINTER MEAL.

Serves 4–6

1 tablespoons extra-virgin olive oil
1 medium onion, diced
4 cloves garlic, minced
4 cups vegetable broth (low-sodium preferred)
1 bunch kale, ribs removed and chopped
2 large carrots, sliced into ¼-inch coins
1 (15-ounce) can Italian-style diced tomatoes
1 (15-ounce) can cannellini beans, drained and rinsed
salt, to taste

In a large, heavy-bottomed pot, cook the onions with olive oil over medium heat for about 3 minutes. Add the garlic and cook for 2 minutes longer. When the onions and garlic are translucent, add the vegetable broth, kale, tomatoes, and carrots, then cover. Cook until the carrots and kale are tender, about 15-20 minutes. When the carrots and kale are tender, add the cannellini beans, salt to taste, and cook until the beans are heated through.

Per 1-cup serving: 419 calories, 4.7g fat (1g saturated fat), 0mg cholesterol, 947mg sodium, 68.7g carbs, 24.1g dietary fiber, 9.1g sugar, 26.9g protein

MAYOCOBA BEAN SOUP

MAYOCOBA. ALREADY SOUNDS DELICIOUS, NO? ACCORDING TO *COOK'S THESAURUS,* MAYOCOBA BEANS ARE ALSO CALLED PERUVIAN, CANARY, OR PERUANO BEANS, AND CAN BE SUBSTITUTED FOR PINTO BEANS AND VICE VERSA. I LIKE USING THE MAYOCOBAS IN THIS RECIPE BECAUSE THEY BLEND INTO A BEAUTIFUL, WARM-HUED SOUP THAT IS SILKY-SPECTACULAR.

Serves 4–6

2 cloves garlic, minced
1 teaspoon extra-virgin olive oil
1 (32-ounce) can mayocoba beans, liquid reserved (use pinto beans if you
can't find mayocoba beans)
1 (8-ounce) can diced tomatoes
salt, to taste
Tabasco sauce, to taste

In a medium pot, sauté the garlic in a teaspoon of olive oil for 1–2 minutes, and then add the remaining ingredients (beans and tomatoes) and let simmer for 10 minutes.

One small batch at a time, add the mixture to a blender and blend until smooth. Transfer the blended soup back to the pot and return to a simmer. Add salt and Tabasco to taste. If you wish, garnish the soup with Tofutti sour cream and chives as pictured.

Per 1-cup serving: 130 calories, 1.6g fat (0.1g saturated fat), 0mg cholesterol, 1,065mg sodium, 20.8g carbs, 6.8g dietary fiber, 2.4g sugar, 6.7g protein

ITALIAN WHITE BEAN SOUP

JAWS DROPPED WHEN I SERVED THIS TO THE COOKBOOK TEAM DURING OUR RECIPE TESTING PHASE. THEY HAD THE RECIPE RIGHT IN FRONT OF THEM—IT WAS ONLY 5 INGREDIENTS LONG (MINUS THE WATER), SO EXPECTATIONS WEREN'T VERY HIGH. ALL PRECONCEIVED NOTIONS CHANGED WITH ONE CREAMY, ROSEMARY-SCENTED SPOONFUL. YES, IT IS THAT GOOD.

Serves 4–6

1 teaspoon extra-virgin olive oil
2 cloves garlic, minced
1 cup water (add more for preferred consistency)
1 (32-ounce) can Great Northern beans, liquid reserved
1-2 teaspoons McKay's Chicken Style Instant Broth and Seasoning (or other chicken-like seasoning)
1 teaspoon fresh rosemary, stem removed and leaves chopped

In a medium pot, sauté the garlic in olive oil for 2-3 minutes. When the garlic is translucent, add the remaining ingredients and simmer for 10 minutes.

Per 1-cup serving: 188 calories, 2.5g fat (0.2g saturated fat), 0mg cholesterol, 147mg sodium, 33g carbohydrates, 13g dietary fiber, 1.6g sugar, 8.1g protein

RUSTIC TOMATO, RICE & KALE STEW

THIS IS AN EVERYTHING-BUT-THE-KITCHEN-SINK STEW, BUT WE FIGURED THAT INCLUDING ADDING THE KITCHEN SINK MIGHT NOT MAKE THE MOST POSITIVE FIRST IMPRESSION. GRAIN, VEGETABLES, AND STARCH... THIS HAS IT ALL. THE ADDITION OF BLACK BEANS, IF YOU HAVE A CAN IN YOUR PANTRY, WOULD ONLY SERVE TO BALANCE IT FURTHER, NO?

Serves 4–6

1¼ cups brown rice, cooked
1 (28-ounce) can fire-roasted tomatoes
3 cups vegetable broth, divided (low-sodium preferred)
¾ cup nutritional yeast flakes
1 bunch kale, ribs removed and julienned
3 red potatoes, diced
2 cups frozen vegetable blend
2 bay leaves
1 tablespoon chili powder
1 teaspoon garlic powder (or 2 cloves minced fresh garlic)
cayenne pepper, to taste
salt, to taste

Prepare the rice according to package instructions.

While the rice is cooking, add the fire-roasted tomatoes and 1 cup of vegetable broth to a high-speed blender, then blend on low until smooth. Pour the mixture into a large, heavy-bottomed pot. Add the potatoes and 2 cups of vegetable broth to the pot and boil until the potatoes are fork tender, about 10-15 minutes.

Add the frozen vegetables and seasonings (bay leaves, chili powder, garlic, powder, cayenne, and salt), and reduce the heat to a simmer. When the vegetables are cooked through, add the kale and cooked rice. Season to taste, adding more spice and salt if desired.

Simmer on low until the kale is tender, at least 10 minutes. Finally, remove the bay leaves and serve.

Per 1-cup serving: 214 calories, 2g fat (0.3 g saturated fat), 0mg cholesterol, 570mg sodium, 40g carbs, 11g dietary fiber, 9g sugar, 12g protein

SPICY 3-BEAN CHILI

YOU'LL NEVER MISS THE MEAT IN THIS BEAN PROTEIN-PACKED CHILI. SPOON DOLLOPS OF IT ON TOP OF A STEAMING BAKED POTATO OR SLAB OF CORNBREAD. EAT IT WITH CHIPS IN PLACE OF SALSA. MAKE A BREAKFAST SCRAMBLE WITH CRUMBLED TOFU AND TORTILLAS. USE IT AS A BURRITO OR TACO FILLING... OR SIMPLY EAT IT THE WAY I DO: WITH A SPOON AND THE HEEL OF A BAGUETTE.

Serves 6–8

2 tablespoons extra-virgin olive oil

2 cups onion, chopped

4 cloves garlic, minced

1 red bell pepper, chopped

2 tablespoons chili powder (reduce for a less spicy chili)

2 teaspoons dried oregano

1½ teaspoons ground cumin

½ teaspoon cayenne pepper

1 (15-ounce) can black beans, drained and ½ cup liquid reserved

1 (15-ounce) can kidney beans, drained and rinsed

1 (15-ounce) can chickpeas, drained and rinsed

1 (15-ounce) can fire-roasted tomato sauce

salt, to taste

2 tablespoons cilantro, chopped (optional)

Heat olive oil in a large pot over medium-high heat and add the onions, garlic, and bell peppers. Sauté until the onions are translucent and soft, about 10 minutes.

Add the seasonings (chili powder, oregano, cumin, and cayenne) and stir for 2 minutes. Then, add the tomato sauce, beans, and ½ cup of reserved black bean liquid. Bring the chili to a boil, stirring occasionally.

When the chili has reached a boil, reduce the heat to medium low and simmer until flavors blend and thicken to your liking, at least 15 minutes. Season to taste with salt to taste, then top with chopped cilantro, if desired.

Per 1-cup serving: 192 calories, 5g fat (1g saturated fat), 609mg sodium, 32g carbs, 9g dietary fiber, 5g sugar, 9g protein

FEIJOADA (BRAZILIAN BLACK BEAN STEW)

FEIJOADA IS A CLASSIC BRAZILIAN DISH, AN ALL-DAY SORT OF STAPLE THAT COMES FROM THE SAME FAMILY AS FRENCH CASSOULETS AND AMERICAN BAKED BEANS. WHILE THERE ARE AS MANY VERSIONS AS THERE ARE COOKS IN BRAZIL, THE BASIC ELEMENTS OF THE DISH ARE ALWAYS THE SAME: BLACK BEANS AND AN ASSORTMENT OF VEGETABLES. TRADITIONALLY, A HODGEPODGE OF CURED MEATS ARE THROWN INTO THE MIX, BUT OUR VERSION UPS THE VEG-CONTENT INSTEAD.

A SURPRISING ASPECT OF FEIJOADA IS THE ORANGE. THE HABIT OF SERVING SLICED ORANGES WITH FEIJOADA MAY SEEM UNUSUAL IF YOU'VE NEVER TRIED IT, BUT THE JUICY TANG OF THE CITRUS PROVIDES A REFRESHING CONTRAST TO THE RICHNESS OF THE DISH. IT'S WHAT REALLY SETS THIS RECIPE APART FROM A RUN-OF-THE-MILL BEAN SOUP.

Serves 6–8

7 cups water
5 (15-ounce) cans black beans, drained and rinsed
1 (15-ounce) can stewed tomatoes, diced
1 medium onion, diced
2 cloves garlic, minced
2 stalks celery, diced
1 green bell pepper, diced
½ teaspoon dried oregano
1 teaspoon ground cumin
salt, to taste

Add all ingredients to a large, heavy-bottomed pot over medium heat. Stir occasionally, until the celery and bell pepper are tender, then serve.

Per 1-cup serving: 235 calories, 2g fat (0g saturated fat), 0mg cholesterol, 570mg sodium, 43g carbs, 15g dietary fiber, 5 sugar, 14g protein

EWALD WILD RICE STEW

THIS CREAMY, THICK, GRAIN-STUDDED STEW IS SO DELICIOUS THAT IT DESERVES THE AUTHOR'S NAME IN THE TITLE. KIMBERLY EWALD, WHO GRACIOUSLY SHARED THIS RECIPE WITH ME, LIVES IN MINNESOTA WHERE WILD RICE IS THE STATE GRAIN AND A PANTRY STAPLE. NEEDLESS TO SAY, KIM IS A WILD RICE AFICIONADO AND THIS STEW IS AN EXCELLENT REPRESENTATION OF THE BLACK GRAIN.

Serves 4–6

½ cup wild rice, uncooked
2 cups water
2 cups unsweetened soy milk
1 cup raw cashews
2 cloves garlic
½ medium onion
¼ cup pearl barley, uncooked
1 cup carrots, shredded
1 teaspoons salt
1 tablespoon McKay's Chicken Style Instant Broth and Seasoning (or other chicken-like seasoning)
½ teaspoon poultry seasoning
1 teaspoon McKay's Beef Style Instant Broth and Seasoning (or other beef-like seasoning)
1 tablespoon Bragg Liquid Aminos

Cook the wild rice according to the package's instructions. When the rice begins to soften and crack, take it off the heat, drain, and set aside.

While the rice is cooking, use a high-speed blender to blend the cashews, garlic, onions, and some of the water (enough to liquefy the other ingredients).

Transfer the cashew cream to a large pot over medium heat. Add the remaining water, uncooked barley, cooked wild rice, shredded carrots, and the remaining seasonings (salt, McKay's Chicken Style seasoning, poultry seasoning, beef style seasoning, and Bragg Liquid Aminos).

Simmer for a couple hours, or until the barley is cooked and chewy and the stew has reduced to a thick, porridge-like consistency.

Per 1-cup serving: 246 calories, 10g fat (1.5g saturated fat), 0mg cholesterol, 921mg sodium, 32g carbs, 4g dietary fiber, 5g sugar, 9g protein

INDIAN RED LENTIL SOUP

LENTIL SOUP IS USUALLY EATEN WHEN ONE IS IN NEED OR WANT OF SOMETHING COMFORTING AND INEXPENSIVE. THIS VARIATION IS MUCH THE SAME, EXCEPT WITH THE ADDED BONUS OF BEING QUITE EXOTIC IN FLAVOR, TOO. THE FRAGRANT INDIAN SPICES LIGHTEN AND BRIGHTEN THE SOUP'S HOMEY FLAVOR. RED LENTILS TEND TO EASILY BREAK DOWN INTO A COARSE PUREE DURING THE COOKING PROCESS, SO YOU SHOULD EXPECT A CREAMIER TEXTURE THAN TYPICAL LENTIL SOUPS.

Serves 4–6

5 cups water
1 cup red lentils, uncooked
1 clove garlic, crushed
1 tablespoon extra-virgin olive oil
1 cup onions, chopped
½ cup celery, thinly sliced
1 cup carrots, finely diced
1½ tablespoons tomato paste
1 bay leaf
⅛ teaspoon chili powder
1 teaspoon salt
¾ (15-ounce) can tomatoes, chunky, whole-crushed
1 tablespoon curry powder
½ cup parsley or cilantro (optional)

In a large pot, combine the first 7 ingredients (water, red lentils, garlic, olive oil, onions, celery, and carrots) together, and bring to a boil. Reduce the heat to medium and simmer for about 2 hours, making sure to keep the pot covered so the liquid doesn't evaporate.

Except for the parsley, add the rest of the ingredients (tomato paste, bay leaf, chili powder, salt, tomatoes, curry powder) and let simmer for a few minutes longer. Just before serving, stir in the ½ cup of freshly chopped parsley.

Per 1-cup serving: 109 calories, 2g fat (0.3g saturated fat), 0mg cholesterol, 406mg sodium, 18g carbs, 6g dietary fiber, 1.4g sugar, 6g protein

CREAM OF TOMATO SOUP

THE ADDITION OF COCONUT MILK TURNS THIS CREAM OF TOMATO SOUP INTO A SILKY-SPECIAL ONE.

Serves 4–6

1 cup onion, chopped
3 cloves garlic, minced
2 teaspoons extra-virgin olive oil
1 (28-ounce) can diced tomatoes
½ teaspoon salt
2 tablespoons McKay's Chicken Style Instant Broth and Seasoning (or other chicken-like seasoning)
½ teaspoon dried thyme
1½ tablespoons brown sugar
2 cups water
dash of cayenne pepper
1 cup coconut milk

In a large pot over medium heat, sauté the onion and garlic in olive oil until they're soft and translucent, about 3 minutes. Add the remaining ingredients, except the coconut milk, and simmer for 20 minutes.

After 20 minutes, transfer the soup mixture to a high-speed blender. Add the coconut milk and blend until smooth.

Transfer the soup back to the stovetop and heat to your desired temperature.

Per 1-cup serving: 136 calories, 9g fat (6g saturated fat), 0mg cholesterol, 813mg sodium, 14g carbs, 1.2g dietary fiber, 8g sugar, 2g protein

Roasted Peppers & Marinara Sauce

Ground Bulgur "Meat"

Roasted Butternut Squash & Sage

Curried Peas & Almonds

Broccoli with Roasted Peppers & Olives

Roasted Brussels Sprouts

Roasted Root Vegetable Medley

Caramelized Korean Tofu

Chilled Summer Yams

Garlicky Potato & White Bean Mash (left)

Zesty Tomato-Basil Bruschetta

Sweet Baked Lentils

SIDES

ROASTED PEPPERS & MARINARA SAUCE

THIS STUFFED PEPPERS RECIPE FEATURES A BLEND OF MEDITERRANEAN FLAVORS WITH ITS TOMATOES, BASIL, AND CAPERS. IT'S ESPECIALLY GOOD SERVED ALONGSIDE CREAMY FETTUCCINE.

Serves 6–8

3 yellow bell peppers, quartered and seeded
1-2 garlic cloves, diced
1 (8-ounce) can peeled plum tomatoes, chopped, liquid reserved
¼ cup fresh basil leaves, chopped
1-2 tablespoons capers, drained
½ teaspoon extra-virgin olive oil
salt, to taste

Preheat the oven to 350°F. Place the peppers, cut side up, on a baking pan that's been brushed with oil. Roast in the oven for about 20 minutes.

Meanwhile, sauté the garlic over low heat with ½ teaspoon of olive oil in a saucepan until it becomes translucent, about 3 minutes. Add the tomatoes and cook over medium heat for about 15 minutes. Stir occasionally until all of the liquid has evaporated. Add the capers and salt to taste.

Arrange the roasted peppers on a platter and fill with the tomato sauce. Using your fingers, shred the basil and sprinkle atop the peppers and sauce.

Per 2-wedge serving: 50 calories, 0.6g fat (0g saturated fat), 0mg cholesterol, 191mg sodium, 10g carbs, 2g dietary fiber, 3g sugar, 2g protein

GROUND BULGUR "MEAT"

BULGUR IS A QUICK-COOKING TYPE OF WHOLE WHEAT, COMMONLY USED IN MIDDLE EASTERN COOKING, THAT HAS BEEN CLEANED, PARBOILED, DRIED AND GROUND. THIS GROUND BULGUR "MEAT" IS A WONDERFUL STAND-IN FOR GROUND BEEF IN DISHES LIKE TACOS, CHILI, CASSEROLES, AND "MEAT" SAUCES. ONE TIP: IT WORKS ESPECIALLY WELL IN OUR **CORN & GREEN CHILE ENCHILADAS** (P. 106). IF TACO SEASONING ISN'T FOR YOU, TRY MIXING IN YOUR FAVORITE SEASONING!

Makes 6 cups

2 cups bulgur wheat, uncooked
2 cups water
1 cup raw walnuts
1 large onion
2-3 cloves garlic
1 tablespoon McKay's Beef-Like Seasoning (or other beef-like seasoning)
1 teaspoon salt
½ cup water
2 tablespoons taco seasoning (or other preferred seasoning) to be added later

MAKE THE GROUND BURGER: Preheat oven to 300°F. Place bulgur wheat in a saucepan. Process the remaining ingredients (water, walnuts, onion, garlic, McKay's Seasoning, salt) in a high-speed blender until smooth, then pour over the bulgur wheat. Cook over low heat for about 5 minutes, stirring frequently, while simmering. Turn off the heat and let it stand for about 20 minutes.

Spread evenly on a baking sheet covered with parchment paper and bake for about 1 hour, or until the burger is mostly dry. After 30 minutes, stir. When done cooking, remove from oven and crumble it with your fingers. Since this recipe makes a large amount, place the desired portion in a skillet, then add water and seasoning for flavor. Freeze the remaining bulgur in sandwich bags. When ready to use, heat the bulgur meat in a skillet, adding water and desired seasoning.

Per ¼-cup serving: 83 calories, 3.5g fat (0.3g saturated fat), 0mg cholesterol, 173mg sodium, 12g carbs, 3g dietary fiber, 0.2g sugar, 2.5g protein

ROASTED BUTTERNUT SQUASH & SAGE

ROASTED SQUASH EMBODIES THE ESSENCE OF WINTER MEALS AND COULD BE THE PERFECT SOLUTION IF YOU WERE SEARCHING FOR A PLANT-BASED HOLIDAY SIDE DISH. CONSIDER THIS SIMPLE RECIPE A BASE FOR A MORE DRESSED-UP ROASTED SQUASH AND SAGE DISH: CONSIDER ADDING CARAMELIZED ONIONS, DRIED CRANBERRIES, AND TOASTED PINE NUTS FOR A MORE LAVISH HOLIDAY SPREAD.

Makes 4–6 side servings

½ butternut squash, peeled and diced into ½-inch cubes (about 3 cups)
1 tablespoon extra-virgin olive oil
½ teaspoon salt
5-7 leaves fresh sage, chopped (or 2 tablespoons dried sage)

Preheat the oven to 400°F. In a large bowl, combine the squash, olive oil, and salt until the squash is evenly coated. Stir in the sage.

Transfer the squash to a nonstick roasting pan and bake in the oven until the squash is tender and lightly browned, about 20 minutes.

Per ½-cup serving: 63 calories, 2.5g fat (0.4g saturated fat), 0mg cholesterol, 198mg sodium, 11g carbs, 3g dietary fiber, 0g sugar, 1g protein

CURRIED PEAS & ALMONDS

LOOKING FOR A QUICK SIDE DISH THAT WON'T TAKE UP OVEN OR STOVETOP SPACE? THIS RECIPE MIGHT BE YOUR ANSWER. VIBRANT COLORS AND AN EXCITING COMBINATION OF SOFT AND CRUNCHY TEXTURES MAKE THIS CURRIED PEA DISH AN EXCELLENT CHANGE-OF-PACE ADDITION TO ANY MEAL.

Serves 6–8

1 (16-ounce) bag frozen peas
3 ounces Smokehouse Almonds, chopped
⅓ cup red onions, chopped
⅓ cup reduced-fat Vegenaise (or regular Vegenaise)
1 teaspoon curry powder

Steam the peas until barely done for 3-5 minutes. Drain in a colander and stop the cooking process by running cold water over them. Combine the cooled peas with the remaining ingredients in a large bowl Serve chilled.

Per ½-cup serving (with reduced-fat Vegenaise): 145 calories, 9g fat (0.3g saturated fat), 0mg cholesterol, 202mg sodium, 13g carbs, 4g dietary fiber, 4g sugar, 6g protein

BROCCOLI WITH ROASTED PEPPERS & OLIVES

BROCCOLI IS NATIVE TO THE MEDITERRANEAN AND ASIA MINOR, SO IT ONLY SEEMS RIGHT TO PAIR IT WITH MEDITERRANEAN FLAVORS, LIKE SMOKY PEPPERS, ACIDIC OLIVES, AND A KICK OF LEMON. GREEN, RED, PURPLE-BLACK, AND YELLOW--IT'S A BEAUTIFUL PLATE OF BRIGHT AND COMPLEX FLAVORS.

Serves 6–8

½ red bell pepper (about 1 cup), chopped
1 teaspoon extra-virgin olive oil
1 large head of broccoli, cut into florets (about 3 cups chopped)
10 kalamata olives, quartered
1 clove garlic, thinly sliced
2 teaspoons fresh marjoram, finely chopped (or ½ teaspoon dried)
salt, to taste
lemon wedges, for serving

ROAST THE PEPPERS: Preheat the oven to 400°F. Brush both sides of the bell pepper with olive oil and place cut side down on a sheet pan. Roast the red pepper in the oven for 10 minutes. When the pepper has cooled down, peel off the skin and discard. Dice the pepper into small cubes, and set aside.

While the peppers are roasting, steam the broccoli in a bit of water until tender, but still crunchy, then set aside.

Heat oil in a skillet, and sauté the garlic slices over medium heat until they're browned. Add the steamed broccoli, quartered olives, roasted bell pepper, and marjoram, and sauté until vegetables are heated through.

Salt to taste and serve with lemon wedges.

Per ½-cup serving: 62 calories, 4g fat (0.1g saturated fat), 0mg cholesterol, 170mg sodium, 5g carbs, 2g dietary fiber, 0g sugar, 1.5g protein

ROASTED BRUSSELS SPROUTS

THE SECRET TO MAKING BRUSSELS SPROUTS PALATABLE TO JUST ABOUT ANYONE: ROASTING BRUSSELS SPROUTS BRINGS OUT THEIR WONDERFUL NUTTY FLAVOR, PLUS IT'S REALLY EASY TO DO.

Serves 6–8

30 brussels sprouts
1 teaspoon extra-virgin olive oil
¼ teaspoon salt, or to taste
¼ cup pine nuts
¼ cup dried currants or cranberries

Preheat the oven to 400°F. Cut the ends off the brussels sprouts, and take off the flimsiest outer leaves before cutting the sprouts in half. Toss them in a large mixing bowl with the olive oil and salt.

Transfer the sprouts to a baking pan and place them in the oven. Roast until the outer leaves are slightly brown, about 20–30 minutes. During the last 4 minutes of roasting, add the pine nuts and currants to the pan and return to the oven. Then, remove the pan from the oven and transfer to a serving platter. Squeeze fresh lemon juice over the brussels sprouts and serve.

Per ½-cup serving: 101 calories, 5g fat (0.4g saturated fat), 0mg cholesterol, 120mg sodium, 13g carbs, 4g dietary fiber, 6g sugar, 4g protein

ROASTED ROOT VEGETABLE MEDLEY

ACCORDING TO WORLD-RENOWNED HOLISTIC HEALING PIONEER DR. ANDREW WEIL, "ROOT VEGETABLES ARE SOME OF THE MOST OVERLOOKED AND UNDER-APPRECIATED FOODSTUFFS AROUND." BUT THESE NUTRITIONAL STOREHOUSES ARE HIDDEN TREASURES WORTHY OF YOUR NOTICE. NOT ONLY ARE THEY AVAILABLE IN WINTER WHEN OTHER VEGETABLES ARE HARD TO FIND, BUT THEY ARE ALSO VERY INEXPENSIVE. SWITCH UP THE FOLLOWING RECIPE AND TRY EXPERIMENTING WITH TURNIPS, RUTABAGAS, BEETS, PARSNIPS, AND SQUASH VARIETIES.

Serves 8–10

4 carrots, peeled, quartered, and chopped in 2-inch lengths
5 red potatoes, chopped in large cubes
½ large onion, chopped in large pieces
1 sweet potato, chopped in large cubes
1 celery stalk, chopped in 2-inch lengths (optional)
4 cloves garlic, unpeeled
2 sprigs fresh parsley
handful basil, chopped
6 stems fresh thyme (or ¼ dried)
½ teaspoon dried dill
1 tablespoon extra-virgin olive oil, or to taste
salt, to taste

Preheat oven to 425°F. Place all of the chopped ingredients in a large bowl and toss together with the seasonings and olive oil until the vegetables are well coated.

Transfer the vegetables to a roasting pan and place in the oven. Roast for 30 minutes, then carefully turn the vegetables over. Roast again until the vegetables are tender on both sides, about 20 minutes. Salt to taste and serve.

Per ½-cup serving: 91 calories, 1.5g fat (0.2g saturated fat), 0mg cholesterol, 34mg sodium, 18g carbs, 3g dietary fiber, 3g sugar, 2g protein

CARAMELIZED KOREAN TOFU

PAN-FRIED TOFU IS A TRADITIONAL KOREAN SIDE DISH (OR *BANCHAN*) BUT SHARON CHO, WHO SHARED THIS RECIPE WITH ME, TAKES THE CLASSIC FLAVOR PROFILE FURTHER BY CARAMELIZING THE SAUCE IN THE PAN, TOGETHER WITH THE TOFU. THE RESULT? EVERY FLAVOR—FROM THE MAPLE SYRUP TO THE GINGER—IS ENHANCED TENFOLD. THIS IS A CLASSIC DISH REIMAGINED AND MADE MUCH, MUCH BETTER.

Serves 4–6

TOFU:

extra-virgin olive oil
1 (16-ounce) package extra firm tofu, drained and cut into ½-inch thick slices
salt, to taste

SAUCE:

2 tablespoons maple syrup
2 tablespoons Bragg Liquid Aminos (or low-sodium soy sauce)
1 tablespoon green onion, finely sliced
3 cloves garlic, minced
½ teaspoon fresh ginger, minced
¼ teaspoon chili paste (or ¼ jalapeño, seeded and minced)

GARNISH:

2 green onions, finely sliced
½ teaspoon sesame seeds, toasted

PREPARE THE TOFU: Add a splash of oil into a skillet, and place the sliced tofu strips onto the pan, sprinkling lightly with salt. Fry the tofu strips on medium high heat until golden. Flip the strips and lightly sprinkle with salt. Fry until golden, about 5 minutes each side. Leave in the pan.

Meanwhile, prepare the sauce by whisking together the maple syrup, Bragg Liquid Aminos, garlic, ginger, and chili paste in a bowl. Set aside until the tofu segments are golden.

When the tofu is ready, pour the sauce over it, and let it simmer in the pan for a few minutes or until caramelized. Transfer the tofu onto a serving platter and garnish with green onions and sesame seeds.

Per slice: 82 calories, 4.5g fat (0.6g saturated fat), 0mg cholesterol, 308mg sodium, 6g carbs, 1g dietary fiber, 3g sugar, 6g protein

CHILLED SUMMER YAMS

FOR QUITE SOME TIME, I WASN'T SURE WHAT TO CALL THIS RECIPE. *PUMPKIN PIE MASH? PUMPKIN PIE FILLING? SWEET POTATO SALAD?* THEN, I TOOK A BITE AND CLOSED MY EYES. WHAT CAME TO MIND WERE PICNICS, SUMMERTIME, TUPPERWARE CONTAINERS, AND MY HAPPY CHILDREN. HENCE, "CHILLED SUMMER YAMS," PERFECT FOR PACKING INTO A BIG PICNIC BASKET FOR AN OUTDOOR MEAL WITH FAMILY.

Serves 6–8

3 large yams or sweet potatoes, baked
½ teaspoon pure vanilla extract
1 tablespoon brown sugar
½ teaspoon ground cinnamon
¼ teaspoon ground ginger
¼ teaspoon ground nutmeg
¼ teaspoon salt
pinch of ground allspice
pinch of ground cloves
1 cup pecans, coarsely chopped and toasted

Bake the sweet potatoes in the oven at 375°F until they're fork tender, about an hour. While they're baking, chop and toast the pecans, then set aside.

When the sweet potatoes are done, peel them, being careful not to burn your fingers, and drop them into a food processor or high-speed blender. Blend until smooth, adding soy milk as needed to facilitate blending.

In a large bowl, combine the sweet potatoes with the remaining ingredients (vanilla extract, brown sugar, cinnamon, ginger, nutmeg, salt, allspice, and cloves). Mix to combine the ingredients evenly and chill in the refrigerator.

Serve cold, and just before serving, add the toasted pecans.

Per ½-cup serving: 172 calories, 11g fat (1g saturated fat), 0mg cholesterol, 98mg sodium, 19g carbs, 4g dietary fiber, 9g sugar, 3g protein

GARLICKY POTATO & WHITE BEAN MASH

WHEN IS THE LAST TIME YOU MADE MASHED POTATOES WITHOUT ENTIRE SPOONFULS OF BUTTER? THIS RECIPES USES CREAMY WHITE BEANS TO ADD A SILKY TEXTURE TO THE MASH, ALONG WITH A UNIQUE FLAVOR. TRY MIXING UP THE FLAVORS BY ADDING MORE STEAMED AND MASHED VEGETABLES, LIKE CARROTS, CELERY, OR PARSNIPS.

Serves 6–8

1 tablespoon extra-virgin olive oil
1 head garlic, pointed end cut off
5 large Yukon Gold potatoes, peeled, washed, and cubed
1½ cups (3/4 of a 15-ounce can) cannellini beans, drained and mashed
1 teaspoon onion powder
½ teaspoon salt

Preheat the oven to 375°F. Drizzle olive oil over the cut end of the garlic head, wrap completely with foil, and roast in the oven for 30 minutes, or until the cloves are soft enough to squeeze out of its skin.

While the garlic is roasting, prepare the potatoes and beans. Boil the potatoes in salted water until they're fork tender. While the potatoes are boiling, use a potato masher to mash the beans in a large mixing bowl. When the potatoes are ready, add them to the mixing bowl and mash together with the beans, roasted garlic, and onion salt until it reaches your desired consistency. Salt to taste and serve.

Per 1 cup serving: 225 calories, 2g fat (0.3g saturated fat), 0mg cholesterol, 327mg sodium, 46g carbs, 7g dietary fiber, 2g sugar, 6.25g protein

ZESTY TOMATO-BASIL BRUSCHETTA

BRUSCHETTA (PRONOUNCED "BRU-SKET-TA") IS AN ITALIAN ANTIPASTO DATING BACK TO AT LEAST THE 15TH CENTURY. THE PARAMETERS FOR A "PROPER" BRUSCHETTA ARE SIMPLE: GRILLED BREAD + GARLIC + OLIVE OIL + TOPPINGS OF CHOICE. IN THIS RECIPE, WE'RE STICKING CLOSE TO THE MOST WELL-KNOWN TOMATO-BASIL VERSION, BUT WITH A SURPRISING KICK OF CHILI POWDER.

Serves 6–8

1 whole-wheat baguette, sliced
½ teaspoon salt
3 ripe tomatoes, chopped
2 garlic cloves, minced
1 handful fresh basil leaves, chopped
3 tablespoons extra-virgin olive oil
½ teaspoon chili powder
dash of cayenne pepper (optional)
additional salt, to taste

In a medium bowl, stir together the chopped tomatoes, garlic, basil, olive oil, chili powder, cayenne pepper, and salt. Adjust the salt and spices to taste.

Toast the baguette slices on a grill or in a toaster. Brush with a little oil. When ready to serve, spoon the tomato mixture over the toasted baguette and serve immediately.

Per 2-piece serving: 73 calories, 6.2g fat (0.9g saturated fat), 0mg cholesterol, 196mg sodium, 4.7g carbs, 1.2g dietary fiber, 1.5g sugar, 1g protein

SWEET BAKED LENTILS

THESE BAKED LENTILS MAY REMIND YOU OF THE TYPICAL COMFORT FOOD, AMERICAN BAKED BEANS. TRY THEM ON TOP OF BAKED SWEET POTATOES OR WITH PASTA OR RICE. IF CHEAP, EASY, GOOD FOR YOU, AND FULL OF FLAVOR SOUND LIKE THE RIGHT INGREDIENTS, READ ON.

Serves 8–10

5 cups water
2 cups brown lentils, uncooked
1 teaspoon salt
1 tablespoon molasses
1 teaspoon extra-virgin olive oil
1 medium onion, chopped
1 (12-ounce) can tomatoes, blended

Preheat the oven to 350°F. In a large pot, boil 5 cups of water and cook the lentils until they're tender, about 20 minutes. When the lentils are soft and have absorbed the water, add the remaining ingredients (salt, molasses, olive oil, onion, tomatoes) and stir to combine.

Transfer the lentils to a baking dish and bake for 60 minutes. Serve over rice or pasta as a main dish, or enjoy as a side dish.

Per ½-cup side serving: 67 calories, 0.5g fat (0.1g saturated fat), 0mg cholesterol, 239mg sodium, 11g carbs, 2g dietary fiber, 2.4g sugar, 4g protein

One-Ingredient Banana Ice Cream
Neapolitan Chia-Banana Parfait
Monkey Shake
AB&J Cookies
Lemon Cornmeal Cookies
Citrus Cream Biscuits
Mango & Coconut Rice
Spiced Pumpkin Pie
Raw German Chocolate Cheesecake
Raw Lemon Cheesecake
Coconut Layer Cake (left)

SWEETS

ONE-INGREDIENT BANANA ICE CREAM

YES, THAT'S RIGHT. CREAMY, SOFT-SERVE STYLE ICE CREAM WITH JUST ONE INGREDIENT—AND NO ICE CREAM MAKER NEEDED! WHAT IS THIS ONE MAGIC INGREDIENT THAT CAN BE WHIPPED INTO PERFECTLY RICH AND SILKY ICE CREAM, WITH NO ADDITIONAL DAIRY, SWEETENERS, OR INGREDIENTS NEEDED WHATSOEVER?

THE GOOD OL' BANANA.

IT TURNS OUT THAT FROZEN BANANAS ARE GOOD FOR MORE THAN JUST DIPPING IN CHOCOLATE. IF YOU FREEZE A BANANA UNTIL SOLID, THEN WHIZ IT UP IN A BLENDER OR FOOD PROCESSOR, IT GETS CREAMY AND A LITTLE GOOEY, JUST LIKE GOOD CUSTARD ICE CREAM. YOU MAY HAVE THOUGHT THAT A BLENDED BANANA WOULD BE FLAKY OR ICY, BUT NO—IT MAKES CREAMY, RICH ICE CREAM.

FEEL FREE TO MIX IN OTHER FLAVORS, LIKE BERRY PUREES, COCOA POWDER, AGAVE NECTAR, OR NUT

BUTTER, THEN TOP WITH YOUR FAVORITE TOPPINGS, LIKE COCONUT FLAKES, CHOCOLATE SHAVINGS, MIXED BERRIES, OR ADDITIONAL NUT BUTTER.

1 overripe medium banana = 1 serving

Peel the banana, chop into 1-inch coins, and freeze them in a plastic bag for at least two hours. When the bananas are frozen, blend them in a food processor or a high-speed blender, scraping down the sides as necessary. Add a little soy milk if the bananas are not blending well. Continue to blend until the bananas reach a soft-serve ice cream-like consistency.

Per medium banana (no topping) serving: 105 calories, 0.4g fat (0.1g saturated fat), 0mg cholesterol, 1mg sodium, 27g carbs, 3.1g dietary fiber, 14.4g sugar, 1.3g protein

NEAPOLITAN CHIA-BANANA PARFAIT

THIS IS AS MUCH A DESSERT AS IT IS A BREAKFAST. SERIOUSLY, WHEN IS THE LAST TIME YOU HAD DESSERT FOR BREAKFAST, AND DIDN'T FEEL GUILTY ABOUT IT? THESE PARFAITS TASTE LIKE A DECADENT FROZEN DESSERT, BUT ONLY INVOLVE LAYERS OF OVERNIGHT CHIA-SEED PUDDING, FROZEN BANANA CREAM, AND AN ARRAY OF MIX-INS (OR YOU CAN ALSO PLOP EVERYTHING IN A BOWL IF YOU PREFER NOT TO LAYER THEM).

Serves 1

⅓ cup rolled oats
1 cup unsweetened soy or almond milk
1 tablespoon chia seeds
1 ripe banana, mashed
¼ teaspoon pure vanilla extract
pinch of salt

RASPBERRY CREAM: 1 frozen banana + 4 fresh raspberries

CHOCOLATE CREAM: 1 frozen banana + 2 teaspoons cocoa powder

OPTIONAL TOPPINGS: chopped fruit, nut butter, unsweetened coconut flakes, toasted nuts, granola, or jam

Mix the ingredients in a bowl and place in the fridge overnight. The next day, layer the chia-banana mixture with raspberry and/or chocolate cream and sprinkle with additional fruit and granola, if desired.

Per parfait (without cream): 280 calories, 8.2g fat (0.6g saturated fat), 0mg cholesterol, 417mg sodium, 50.5g cars, 9.3g dietary fiber, 14.8g sugar, 7.4g protein

MONKEY SHAKE

WHEN IT COMES TO MAKING MILKSHAKES AND SMOOTHIES, PEOPLE USUALLY JUST TOSS IN INGREDIENTS AS THEY GO AND HOPE FOR THE BEST. HOWEVER, SOMETIMES A SHAKE TURNS OUT SO WELL THAT IT SIMPLY DEMANDS TO BE WRITTEN DOWN SO THAT IT CAN BE RE-CREATED, WITH THE SAME RESULTS. THIS IS ONE OF THOSE MILKSHAKES. MADE OF BANANAS, NATURAL PEANUT BUTTER, AND COCOA POWDER, THIS RICH, CREAMY TREAT WILL SATISFY YOUR SWEET TOOTH WITHOUT THE SLUGGISH AFTEREFFECTS OF A TRADITIONAL ICE CREAM SHAKE.

Serves 6–8

3 cups soy milk
½ cup peanut butter
10 Medjool dates, pitted

2 teaspoons carob or cocoa powder
3 ripe bananas
1 teaspoon pure vanilla extract
2-3 cups ice

Add the almonds, soy milk, peanut butter, and pitted dates to a high-speed blender and blend until smooth. Then, add the remaining ingredients and blend until smooth.

Per 1-cup serving: 289 calories, 15g fat (2.7g saturated fat), 0mg cholesterol, 143mg sodium, 32.8g carbs, 5g dietary fiber, 20.4g sugar, 10.5 protein

AB&J COOKIES

ALMOND BUTTER & JAM COOKIES. DISCLAIMER: YOUR CHILDREN WILL LOVE THIS RECIPE. ANY RECIPE THAT INSTRUCTS THEM TO JAM THEIR THUMBS INTO COOKIE DOUGH AND FILL IT WITH JAM IS AN A+ IN THEIR BOOKS. IT'S A COOKIE THAT WILL WIN YOUR HEART, TOO. RASPBERRIES AND ALMONDS ARE A WINNING COMBINATION AND THIS RECIPE IN PARTICULAR HIGHLIGHTS THE FLAVORS BEAUTIFULLY—LIGHTLY SWEET, WITH A BUTTERY ALMOND FLAVOR AND POP OF SWEET RASPBERRY GOODNESS. IF YOU AND YOUR CHILDREN ARE FANS OF PB&J, YOU'LL LOVE THIS COOKIE.

Makes 3 dozen cookies

1 cup raw almonds
1 cup rolled oats
1 cup whole-wheat pastry flour
1 teaspoon cinnamon
pinch of salt
½ cup canola oil
½ cup maple syrup
8 tablespoons raspberry jam

Preheat the oven to 350°F. Place almonds in a food processor and grind into a fine powder. Make sure not to over blend, or it will turn into almond butter. Transfer to a mixing bowl. Then use the food processor to grind the oats into a coarse flour. Combine the oat flour with the cinnamon, salt, almond, and whole wheat flour.

Whip the oil and maple syrup together, then add to the almond-oat flour and mix well. Form into walnut sized balls and place on an oiled cookie sheet. Use your thumb to press down on the center of each ball to make ½-inch indents. Add ¼ teaspoon of raspberry jam to each indent. Place the cookie sheet in the oven and bake for 10-15 minutes.

Per cookie: 60 calories, 1.5g fat (0.1g saturated fat), 0mg cholesterol, 5mg sodium, 10.7g carbs, 1g dietary fiber, 4.7g sugar, 1.3g protein

LEMON CORNMEAL COOKIES

IF YOU'RE LOOKING FOR A DESSERT OTHER THAN CHOCOLATE-CARAMEL-COCONUT-ETC., IMAGINE A LIGHTLY SWEET, SUBTLY TART LEMON CORNMEAL COOKIE WITH A DELICATE CRUNCH OF GRANULATED SUGAR ON TOP, I.E., THIS COOKIE.

Makes 2 dozen cookies

1 cup flour
½ cup yellow cornmeal (whole grain, medium grind is preferred)
¼ teaspoon salt
1 teaspoon baking powder
⅓ cup canola oil
½ cup agave nectar
2 teaspoons lemon zest
1 teaspoon vanilla extract
granulated sugar, to coat (optional)

Preheat oven to 350°F. Combine the dry ingredients (flour, cornmeal, salt, baking powder) in a medium bowl. Make a well in the middle of the dry ingredients and add the oil, agave nectar, lemon zest, and vanilla extract. Combine the dry and wet ingredients and mix to form a crumbly dough.

Form into 1½-inch balls and roll in sugar, if using. Place the cookies on parchment-lined baking sheets, and flatten to 2-inch discs. Bake for 8 minutes, or until the edges are light brown.

Per cookie: 157 calories, 6g fat (0.4g saturated fat), 0mg cholesterol, 89mg sodium, 24g carbs, 0.5g dietary fiber, 11g sugar, 1.5g protein

CITRUS CREAM BISCUITS

USUALLY, BISCUITS TEND TO BE A BIT ON THE DRY SIDE, ESPECIALLY WHEN THEY'RE VEGAN, BUT THESE ARE LOVELY AND TENDER, WITH THE SWEET TARTNESS OF THE LEMON AND ORANGE PEEL SHINING THROUGH. THEY'RE A PERFECT BASE FOR STRAWBERRY SHORTCAKE STACKS IN THE SUMMERTIME.

Makes 16 biscuits

2½ cups flour
2½ teaspoons baking powder
½ cup yellow cornmeal (whole grain, coarse grind preferred)
1 teaspoon salt
½ cup sugar
1 (13.5 ounce) can coconut milk
4 teaspoons lemon peel, grated
4 teaspoons orange peel, grated

Preheat oven to 350°F. In a medium bowl, combine the flour, baking powder, cornmeal, salt, and sugar. Stir in the coconut milk and orange and lemon peel until just combined.

Form into balls and roll in sugar, if using. Place dough balls on a greased cookie sheet and bake in oven for 20-24 minutes or until lightly browned. Cool on rack.

Per biscuit: 158 calories, 4.6g fat (3.8g saturated fat), 0mg cholesterol, 228mg sodium, 27g carbs, 1g dietary fiber, 7g sugar, 3g protein

MANGO & COCONUT RICE

ONE OF THE PLEASURES OF HOME COOKING IS DISCOVERING THAT FAVORITE, LONGED-FOR FOODS ARE NOT SO OUT OF REACH, AFTER ALL. MANGO AND COCONUT RICE IS ONE OF THESE FAVORITE FOODS—A DESSERT TO BE ORDERED WHENEVER POSSIBLE IN THAI RESTAURANTS, BUT NEVER MADE AT HOME. IN FACT, MANGO AND COCONUT RICE IS REALLY SIMPLE TO MAKE, AND SOMEHOW TASTES MUCH BETTER WHEN EATEN, SPOONFUL BY WARM SPOONFUL, AT HOME.

Serves 2–4

1-2 mangoes, peeled and sliced
1 cup jasmine rice, uncooked
½ stick cinnamon (or ¼ teaspoon ground cinnamon)
½ cup water
½ (13.5 ounce) can coconut milk
1 tablespoon sugar
½ tablespoon black sesame seeds, toasted (optional)

Combine the brown rice, water, and salt in a saucepan and bring it to a boil. Cover, turn the heat to low, and let it simmer for 45 minutes. Then, remove from heat and pour in the coconut milk. Fluff the rice, then cover and let it sit for about 20 minutes.

Serve with sliced mangoes and an optional sprinkle of sesame seeds.

Per serving: 280 calories, 8.1g fat (5.4g saturated fat), 0mg cholesterol, 26mg sodium, 48.5g carbs, 3.3g dietary fiber, 16.5g sugar, 3.6g protein

SPICED PUMPKIN PIE

YES, PIE. NO MATTER HOW QUICKLY IT MAKES YOUR MIND TURN TO BUTTER, MILK, EGGS, AND WHIPPED CREAM, PIE EASILY LENDS ITSELF TO VEGAN INTERPRETATION. NEED PROOF? TRY THIS 100 PERCENT VEGAN PUMPKIN PIE, MADE WITHOUT CREAM, EGGS, CONDENSED MILK, OR BUTTER. (IT'S DELICIOUS.)

Serves 10–12

1 8-inch pie crust (whole-wheat preferred)
¾ cup sugar
¾ cup dark brown sugar
¼ cup cornstarch
¾ teaspoon ground cinnamon
¼ teaspoon ground nutmeg
¼ teaspoon ground ginger
¼ teaspoon salt
pinch of ground allspice
pinch of cloves
1 (29 ounce) can pumpkin puree (or 2-3 cups fresh)
½ cup coconut milk
½ cup soy milk
1 teaspoon vanilla extract

Preheat the oven to 425°F. Blend all of the ingredients and transfer the mixture to the prepared pie shell. Bake for 15 minutes, turn the temperature to 350°F, then bake for 35-40 minutes, or until the filling has set.

Per slice: 313 calories, 15.3g fat (3.1g saturated fat), 0mg cholesterol, 256mg sodium, 42g carbs, 4g dietary fiber, 18.5g sugar, 4.1g protein

RAW GERMAN CHOCOLATE CHEESECAKE

FREE OF REFINED SUGAR, GRAINS, GLUTEN, DAIRY, AND EGGS, THIS DECADENT, SILKY-SMOOTH, NUT-BASED CHEESECAKE CONTAINS NO TRICKY INGREDIENTS AND ONLY CONSISTS OF TWO SIMPLE PARTS: A CRUST MADE FROM NUTS AND COCOA, AND A CREAMY CENTER MADE FROM, WELL, NUTS AND COCOA. THE ENTIRE RECIPE CAN BE MADE IN A HIGH-SPEED BLENDER, AND IT'S KIND OF MAGICAL TO SEE THE WAY THE INGREDIENTS TRANSFORM INTO SOMETHING THAT TASTES SO DISTINCTLY LIKE GERMAN CHOCOLATE CHEESECAKE. I WON'T DENY THAT THIS IS AN INCREDIBLY RICH CAKE, SO MAKE SURE TO BE MINDFUL OF PORTION SIZES!

Serves 24

CRUST:

1¾ cups raw almonds
¼ cup raw cacao powder
¾ cup Medjool dates, pitted
1 teaspoon pure vanilla extract
⅛ teaspoon salt
2 tablespoons agave nectar

FILLING:

3 cups raw cashews
1½ cups almond or soy milk
1 cup agave nectar
5 tablespoons raw cacao powder
2 tablespoons pure vanilla extract
¼ teaspoon salt
3 tablespoons soy lecithin
1¼ cups coconut butter or oil, melted

MAKE THE CRUST: Add all crust ingredients to a food processor. Process until the crust begins to rise on the sides of the processor's bowl. Stop the machine and use a spatula to mix the crust. Repeat a few times until the mixture is smooth and consistent. The final result should be a mixture that holds together with gentle pressure.

Wash your hands so the crust doesn't stick, then use your knuckles to lightly and evenly press the mixture into the bottom portion only of a 9-inch cheesecake pan. Set aside.

MAKE THE FILLING: Blend all filling ingredients except the soy lecithin and coconut oil, until the mixture is completely creamy. Then, add the lecithin and melted coconut oil. Blend on high until well mixed.

Pour the filling over the crust and tap the cheesecake pan on the counter several times to remove air bubbles in the filling. Refrigerate overnight or in the freezer for 2 hours. To store, cover and place in the fridge. The cheesecake keeps well for at least 4 days.

Per slice: 267 calories, 17g fat (8g saturated fat), 0mg cholesterol, 48mg sodium, 26g carbs, 4g dietary fiber, 18g sugar, 5g protein

RAW LEMON CHEESECAKE

ANOTHER NOT-SO-ORDINARY CHEESECAKE THAT IS RAW, AND FREE OF DAIRY, GLUTEN, AND EGGS! NO, THIS IS DEFINITELY NOT YOUR ORDINARY CHEESECAKE—IT'S A ROUND MOLD OF SERENDIPITOUS DELICIOUSNESS! THE CRUST, GROUND ALMONDS, COCONUT FLAKES, AND FRESH LEMON JUICE, ADDS A SATISFYING CRUNCH. THE "CHEESE," COMPOSED OF MORE FRESH LEMON, CASHEWS, AGAVE NECTAR, AND COCONUT OIL, LENDS THE CREAMIEST, SMOOTHEST TEXTURE. A HIGH-PROTEIN AND RATHER WONDERFUL ALTERNATIVE TO TRADITIONAL CHEESECAKE, THIS TREAT, SERVED IN SMALL PORTIONS, IS A GO-TO DESSERT FOR SPECIAL OCCASIONS OR JUST FOR A GLOOMY DAY WHEN YOU'RE IN NEED OF SOMETHING CHEERFUL AND BRIGHT.

Serves 24

CRUST:

1 cup almond slivers
1 cup unsweetened coconut flakes
1 tablespoon fresh lemon juice
1 tablespoon agave nectar
pinch of salt

FILLING:

3 cups raw cashews
1½ cups unsweetened almond milk
1 cup lemon juice, fresh
1 cup coconut oil, melted
½ cup agave nectar
1 teaspoon pure vanilla extract
¼ teaspoon salt
1 tablespoon soy lecithin (optional)
1 teaspoon lemon zest (optional)

MAKE THE CRUST: Blend the almonds, coconut, and salt in a food processor until a flour-like consistency is achieved. Then, add the agave nectar and lemon juice and process until the mixture sticks together. Press the mixture into a 9-inch springform pan.

MAKE THE FILLING: Blend all ingredients except the lecithin and coconut oil in a high-speed blender, until completely creamy. Add the lecithin and melted coconut oil, and blend on high until well mixed. Pour the filling over the crust and let it firm up in the fridge overnight.

Per slice: 230 calories, 19g fat (11g saturated fat), 0mg cholesterol, 54mg sodium, 15g carbs, 1.4g dietary fiber, 9g sugar, 4g protein

COCONUT LAYER CAKE

WHILE ALL CAKES HAVE THEIR OWN DELICIOUS MERIT, LAYER CAKES ARE SPECIAL. THEY REQUIRE NOT ONLY MASTERING THE ART OF CAKE BAKING, BUT ALSO THE TIME TO BAKE, FROST, STACK, AND FROST AGAIN. MY OPINION? COCONUT CAKE—ESPECIALLY THIS SWEETLY TROPICAL VERSION—IS COMPLETELY WORTH IT.

Serves 16

CAKE:

2 cups all-purpose flour
1 teaspoon baking powder
1 teaspoon baking soda
½ teaspoon salt
½ cup canola oil
2 cups coconut milk
1 cup sugar
2 teaspoons pure vanilla extract
½ teaspoon almond extract (optional)
¾ cup unsweetened shredded coconut

FROSTING:

¼ cup non-hydrogenated margarine, room temperature
¼ cup coconut, soy, or almond milk
1 teaspoon pure vanilla extract
¼ teaspoon pure almond extract (optional)
2 cups confectioners' sugar
1 cup unsweetened shredded coconut

Preheat the oven to 350°F. Grease two nine-inch round pans and dust with flour.

MAKE THE CAKE: In a large bowl, sift together the flour, baking powder, baking soda, and salt. In a separate bowl mix together oil, coconut milk, vanilla, almond extract and sugar. Pour into the dry ingredients and beat until smooth. Stir in 1 cup of the shredded coconut. Pour into prepared cake pans. Bake until the cake is slightly golden and an inserted toothpick comes out clean, about 25 minutes. Let the cakes sit for 10 minutes then remove from pans and place on a cooling rack.

MAKE THE FROSTING: Cream together margarine, coconut milk, vanilla extract, almond extract, and sugar with a handheld mixer until smooth. Add the unsweetened coconut and mix.

Frost the two-layer cake when completely cool. Sprinkle additional coconut flakes on top with a few berries for color, then cut into slices and serve.

Per slice: 443 calories, 27g fat (14g saturated fat), 0mg cholesterol, 216mg sodium, 48g carbs, 3g dietary fiber, 32g sugar, 3.5g protein

SAUCES, DIPS & DRESSINGS

FRESH CORN-BASIL SALSA

FOR OBVIOUS, BASIL-AND-CORN-RELATED REASONS, THIS SALSA IS BEST ON WONDERFULLY HOT SUMMER DAYS.

Makes 2½ cups

5 ears fresh white corn, shucked (or 1 bag frozen white petite corn)
½ cup red onion, finely diced
2 tablespoons fresh lime juice
1 teaspoon extra-virgin olive oil
½ teaspoon salt
½ cup fresh basil leaves, julienned
1 jalapeño, seeded and finely diced, or to taste

Bring a large pot of water to a boil, add the shucked corn, and boil for 3 minutes. While the corn is boiling, prepare a large bowl of ice water. After 3 minutes, drain the corn, then immerse it in icy water to halt the cooking process. When the corn is cool, cut the corn kernels off the cob.

Combine the corn with remaining ingredients and serve.

Per ¼-cup serving: 88 calories, 1.7g fat (0.2g saturated fat), 0mg cholesterol, 159mg sodium, 18g carbs, 3g dietary fiber, 3g sugar, 3.2g protein

MANGO-LIME SALSA

WE LOVE THIS SWEET AND TANGY SALSA BEST WITH THE **CARIBBEAN BURRITOS** (P. 112) BUT IT WOULD BE JUST AS GOOD WITH A SIMPLE HANDFUL OF TORTILLA CHIPS OR ATOP AN ENCHILADA FOR A TROPICAL SPIN ON A FAMILIAR DISH.

Makes 2 cups

2 ripe mangoes, peeled, seeded, and diced into ¼-inch cubes
1½ tablespoons jalapeño pepper, seeded and minced
1 tablespoon shallot, minced
¼ cup fresh cilantro, coarsely chopped
2 tablespoons fresh lime juice
½ teaspoon salt

Toss gently to combine all ingredients.

Per ¼-cup serving: 36 calories, 0.3g fat (0g saturated fat), 0mg cholesterol, 149mg sodium, 9.4g carbs, 1.1g dietary fiber, 7.9g sugar, 0.3g protein

TOMATO-AVOCADO SALSA

A DELICIOUS CROSS BETWEEN GUACAMOLE AND SALSA.

Makes 1½ cups

⅓ cup tomato, seeded and diced
½ avocado, diced
2 tablespoons red onion, chopped
2-3 tablespoons cilantro, chopped
1 tablespoon jalapeño, seeded and diced
1 tablespoon fresh lemon juice
⅛ teaspoon salt, to taste

Mix all ingredients and season to taste with salt.

Per ¼-cup serving: 53 calories, 4.5g fat (0.6g saturated fat), 0mg cholesterol, 29mg sodium, 4g carbs, 2.2g dietary fiber, 0.2g sugar, 1g protein

LEMONY AVOCADO DIP

SO MUCH MORE THAN A DIP (ALTHOUGH IT'S DELICIOUS WITH CHIPS!). I ESPECIALLY LOVE THIS AS A DRESSING FOR KALE SALADS.

Serves 2–4

1 avocado, peeled
1 lemon, juiced
½ teaspoon salt

Using a fork, mash all ingredients together.

Per 4-tablespoon serving: 169 calories, 14.8g fat (2.2g saturated fat), 0mg cholesterol, 589mg sodium, 11.3g carbs, 7.5g dietary fiber, 1.4g sugar, 2.3g protein

HUMMUS

HUMMUS IS A LONG-TIME FAVORITE IN MY HOUSE, AND A GO-TO WHENEVER I NEED TO BRING SOMETHING TO A DINNER PARTY WITH MINIMAL EFFORT. THIS HUMMUS RECIPE IS ONE OF MANY, BUT ITS CREAMINESS AND DELICATE FLAVOR ENHANCED BY THE CUMIN HAS CONSISTENTLY BROUGHT PRAISE FROM MANY FRIENDS AND ACQUAINTANCES FOR BEING THE "MOST AUTHENTIC" THEY'D EVER TASTED.

Makes 3 cups

1 (15-ounce) can chickpeas, drained, rinsed, ¼ cup liquid reserved
½ cup tahini
¼ cup extra-virgin olive oil (low fat option: try 2 tablespoons instead)
1 clove garlic
1 tablespoon ground cumin
juice of 1 lemon
⅓ cup water, or as needed
salt, to taste

Place all ingredients except the water into a food processor or high-speed blender. Blend until smooth, adding as much water as needed to reach the preferred consistency. Taste and add more garlic, salt, lemon juice, or cumin as needed. To serve, sprinkle lightly with cumin.

Per 2-tablespoon serving: 103 calories, 10g fat (1.4g saturated fat), 0mg cholesterol, 109mg sodium, 2.9g carbs, 1.1g dietary fiber, 0.2g sugar, 1.9g protein

SIMPLE BASIL PESTO

I ADORE FRESH PESTO. IT IS SO EASY TO MAKE AND BRINGS INCREDIBLE FLAVOR TO EVERYTHING: PASTA, SANDWICHES, GRILLED VEGETABLES, RICE, PIZZA, ETC. IT'S AN ADDITION OF SOMETHING LOVELY WITHOUT FAIL. TRADITIONAL PESTO CALLS FOR PARMESAN CHEESE, BUT THIS ONE SIMPLY OMITS IT AND UPS THE ANTE WITH EXTRA PINE NUTS AND LEMON. BESIDES, SHOULDN'T THE BASIL BE THE STAR?

Makes 3 cups

1 cup pine nuts
½ cup extra-virgin olive oil
⅓ cup water (depending on desired consistency)
¼ cup fresh lemon juice
1½ cups fresh basil
1-2 garlic cloves
1 teaspoon salt

Blend all ingredients in a blender until smooth.

Per ¼-cup serving: 152 calories, 16.2g fat (1.8g saturated fat), 0mg cholesterol, 158mg sodium, 2g carbs, 0.5g dietary fiber, 0.5g sugar, 1.7g protein

PISTACHIO-BASIL SPREAD

IT'S A HIGH CLAIM BUT...YOU CAN NEVER GO WRONG WITH PESTO. THIS EXCEPTIONALLY FLAVORFUL VERSION USES PISTACHIOS INSTEAD OF PINE NUTS AND TASTES INCREDIBLE WITH CRACKERS AS AN APPETIZER, TOSSED TOGETHER WITH PASTA, SPREAD ON SANDWICHES AND BURGERS, AND EVEN BETWEEN LAYERS OF LASAGNAS OR CASSEROLES.

Makes 1¼ cups

1-2 garlic cloves
1 cup unsalted pistachios, shelled
1 cup fresh basil, loosely packed
1 teaspoon fresh lemon juice
¼ teaspoon salt
¼ cup extra-virgin olive oil

Add all ingredients except olive oil to a food processor. Pulse until nuts are finely chopped. Gradually, add the olive oil through a food chute.

Per 2-tablespoon serving: 94 calories, 8g fat (1g saturated fat), 0mg cholesterol, 59mg sodium, 4g carbs, 1.4g dietary fiber, 1g sugar, 3g protein

LEMON-GINGER DRESSING

THANKS TO MY MOM, I WAS INTRODUCED TO THIS OIL-FREE DRESSING THAT MANAGES TO MAINTAIN ALL THE BRIGHTNESS AND ACIDITY THAT I LOVE IN A DRESSING.

Makes ½ cup

6 tablespoons fresh lemon juice
4 tablespoons maple syrup
2 tablespoon fresh ginger, grated

Combine all ingredients.

Per ¼-cup serving: 134 calories, 0.8g fat (0.5g saturated fat), 0mg cholesterol, 14mg sodium, 31.6g carbs, 0.9g dietary fiber, 25g sugar, 0.9g protein

AGAVE-ORANGE SALAD DRESSING

NOT ALL SALAD DRESSINGS HAVE TO BE OIL-AND-VINEGAR ONES. THIS DRESSING WILL TAKE CRISP AND REFRESHING SALADS TO A WHOLE NEW LEVEL, ADDING A CITRUSY, TANGY, AND SLIGHTLY SWEET NOTE TO ANY BED OF GREENS. I LIKE IT BEST ON FRESH CHOPPED ROMAINE LETTUCE.

Makes ½ cup

½ orange or 1 mandarin orange, peeled
2 tablespoons fresh lemon juice
2 tablespoons agave nectar
pinch of salt

Blend until smooth.

Per tablespoon serving: 21 calories, 0g fat (0g saturated fat), 0mg cholesterol, 20mg sodium, 6g carbs, 0.3g dietary fiber, 5g sugar, 0.1g protein

THOUSAND ISLAND DRESSING

WHERE I LIVE IN CALIFORNIA IS HOME TO A WORLD-FAMOUS BURGER SHOP CALLED IN-N-OUT. THEY MAKE SIMPLE BURGERS—TOASTED BUN, BURGER, TOMATO, LETTUCE, ONION, ETC.—BUT THE SECRET TO THEIR SUCCESS IS THAT INSTEAD OF KETCHUP AND MUSTARD, THEY USE THOUSAND ISLAND DRESSING. I SAY ALL OF THIS TO TELL ANYONE WHO'S TRIED AND LOVED THIS BURGER THAT YOU CAN RE-CREATE THIS BURGER AT HOME—BUT WITH ALL PLANT-BASED INGREDIENTS! THIS THOUSAND ISLAND DRESSING IS COMPLETELY VEGAN (AS LONG AS YOU GET VEGAN WORCESTERSHIRE AND IS GREAT ON BURGERS, SANDWICHES, AS DIP, AND OF COURSE, ON SALADS.

Makes 1 cup

1 cup reduced-fat Vegenaise
⅓ cup ketchup
1 clove garlic
2 tablespoons fresh lemon juice
⅓ cup sweet pickle relish
pinch of cayenne pepper
pinch of salt
splash of vegan Worcestershire sauce (optional)

Mix all ingredients to combine.

Per 2 tablespoon serving: 86 calories, 8g fat (0g saturated fat), 0mg cholesterol, 270mg sodium, 5g carbs, 3g sugar, 0g protein

LEMON-GARLIC VINAIGRETTE

DON'T BUY BOTTLED DRESSING WITH COUNTLESS INGREDIENTS; JUST TRY THIS ONE! LEMON AND GARLIC BRING A WORLD OF ZING AND YUM TO ANY SALAD, FANCY OR PLAIN.

Makes ½ cup

½ teaspoon lemon zest
3 tablespoons fresh lemon juice
¼ teaspoon salt
1 clove garlic, minced
3 tablespoons water
2 tablespoons extra-virgin olive oil

Combine all ingredients except the oil (lemon zest and juice, salt, garlic, and water). Then, slowly add the oil, whisking it until it's fully combined with the rest of the ingredients.

Per 1/4-cup serving: 128 calories, 14.2g fat (2.2g saturated fat), 0mg cholesterol, 296mg sodium, 1.1g carbs, 0.5g sugar, 0.3g protein

BASIC CREAM SAUCE

THE MOST VERSATILE OF OUR CREAM SAUCES, YOU MAY HAVE NOTICED THIS RECIPE POP UP IN MANY OF OUR OTHER RECIPES. CASHEW CREAM IS THE RESULT OF SOAKING CASHEWS AND BLENDING THEM WITH WATER. DEPENDING ON HOW MUCH WATER YOU ADD, IT CAN QUITE THICK— LIKE THE TEXTURE OF RICOTTA—OR THIN ENOUGH TO RESEMBLE HEAVY CREAM. IT DEMANDS VERY LITTLE EFFORT AND IT'S EXTREMELY VERSATILE. ADD SOME MAPLE SYRUP OR DEMERARA SUGAR, AND IT BECOMES A SWEET DESSERT CREAM. ADD SOME ONION POWDER AND MCKAY'S SEASONING AND THE CREAM SAUCE TURNS SAVORY. IN THE FOLLOWING RECIPE, BASIC CASHEW CREAM MEETS RICH, SAVORY INGREDIENTS THAT, COMBINED WITH CORNSTARCH, TURN INTO A LUSCIOUS SAUCE FOR ANY NUMBER OF YOUR FAVORITE DINNERS.

Makes 4 cups

1 cup raw cashews
4 cups water, divided
1 teaspoon salt, or more to taste
2 teaspoons onion powder
1 tablespoon McKay's Chicken Style Instant Broth and Seasoning (or other chicken-like seasoning)
½ teaspoon garlic powder (optional)
2 tablespoons cornstarch or flour

Starting with 2 cups of water, place the rest of the ingredients in a high-speed blender and blend on high for about 2 minutes until smooth. Add the remaining water to the blender, swish it around, and transfer it to a saucepan.

Bring the mixture to a boil, stirring constantly to prevent lumping. As soon as it thickens, remove it from the heat. If a thicker sauce is needed, return it to the heat and slowly stir in more cornstarch, dissolved in cold water, letting the mixture come to a gentle boil as the mixture thickens.

TIP: Add a sprinkle of red pepper flakes for some heat

Per ¼-cup serving: 45 calories, 3g fat (0.5g saturated fat), 0mg cholesterol, 233mg sodium, 4g carbs, 0.3g dietary fiber, 0.8g sugar, 1.3g protein

NACHO CHEESE-STYLE SAUCE

ONE OF THE THINGS I LOVE ABOUT A CHEESE SAUCE IS THAT IT'S COMFORTING AND CREAMY. THIS VEGAN VERSION OF NACHO CHEESE ISN'T NECESSARILY A CARBON COPY OF THE REAL THING, BUT IT DEFINITELY GIVES ME (AND, I HOPE, YOU) THAT SAME KIND OF COMFORTING FEELING WHEN EATEN.

Makes 7 cups

3 cups white potatoes, peeled and chopped
⅓ cup carrots, sliced
½ cup raw cashews
⅓ cup mild olive oil
½ cup nutritional yeast flakes
1 teaspoon onion powder
½ teaspoon garlic powder
2-3 teaspoons salt
dash of turmeric, for color
2 cups water
2 tablespoons non-hydrogenated margarine

Boil the carrots and potatoes until they're fork tender. While the vegetables are cooking, place the cashews and olive oil in a high-speed blender with a small amount of water (just enough to liquefy) and blend until creamy. Add cooked potatoes, carrots, seasonings (nutritional yeast flakes, onion powder, garlic powder, salt, turmeric), and 2 cups of water to the blender, then blend until smooth. Add the margarine and blend until smooth.

Per ¼-cup serving: 64 calories, 4.3g fat (0.7g saturated fat), 0mg cholesterol, 178mg sodium, 5g carbs, 1.2g dietary fiber, 0.5g sugar, 2g protein

CASHEW CHEESE SAUCE

THIS CHEESE-STYLE SAUCE IS STRIKING. IT HAS SUN-DRIED TOMATOES, GARLIC, CASHEWS, AND A SQUEEZE OF LEMON. THE RESULT IS CREAMY, BRIGHT IN COLOR, AND HAS THE STRONG FLAVOR OF SUN-DRIED TOMATOES WITHOUT BEING OVERPOWERING.

Makes 2 cups

1 cup raw cashews
1 cup water
¼ cup sun-dried tomatoes
1 clove garlic, chopped
3 tablespoons fresh lemon juice
3 tablespoons nutritional yeast flakes
1 tablespoon onion flakes
½ tablespoons salt

Add all ingredients to a high-speed blender and blend until the sauce is creamy.

Per ¼-cup serving: 120 calories, 8.3g fat (1.7g saturated fat), 0mg cholesterol, 481mg sodium, 9g carbs, 1.8g dietary fiber, 1.9g sugar, 4.7g protein

CREAMY ALFREDO SAUCE

IT'S HARD TO BEAT A RICH AND CREAMY ALFREDO SAUCE OVER FRESH PASTA. IT'S ALSO SOMETHING THAT YOU MAY HAVE RULED OUT IN YOUR VEGAN JOURNEY. FORTUNATELY, THE CREAMY, SMOOTH FLAVOR OF ALFREDO IS A TASTE THAT CAN BE REPLICATED WITHOUT THE ADDITION OF DAIRY PRODUCTS. NOT ONLY THAT, THIS SAUCE CAN BE WHIPPED TOGETHER IN LESS THAN 15 MINUTES.

Makes 2 cups

1 (16-ounce) package silken tofu
1½ cups unsweetened almond milk
2 cloves garlic
3 tablespoons nutritional yeast flakes
1½ teaspoons fresh lemon juice
1½ teaspoons onion powder
1½ teaspoons salt
2 tablespoons Italian parsley (for garnish)

Blend all ingredients except parsley in a high-speed blender until creamy. Transfer the mixture to a medium saucepan and cook at medium-high heat, stirring constantly so that it does not burn. Sprinkle the parsley on top and serve.

Per ¼-cup serving: 106 calories, 8.9g fat (6.7g saturated fat), 0mg cholesterol, 302mg sodium, 3.9g carbs, 1.7g dietary fiber, 1.4g sugar, 5g protein

BRAZIL NUT GRAVY

BRAZIL NUTS AREN'T USUALLY A PANTRY STAPLE, BUT EVERY TIME I GET MY HANDS ON THEM, I'M PLEASANTLY REMINDED OF HOW BUTTERY AND SWEET THEY TASTE. ALL THE BRAZIL NUT'S AMAZING FLAVORS ARE BROUGHT OUT IN THIS GRAVY RECIPE, SHARED WITH US BY DR. LORAYNE BARTON. WE LIKE IT BEST OVER TOAST FOR BREAKFAST.

Makes 2 cups

1½ cup water, divided
⅔ cup Brazil nuts
1 tablespoon onion powder
3 tablespoons cornstarch
1 tablespoon nutritional yeast flakes
1½ tablespoon Bragg Liquid Aminos (or low-sodium soy sauce)
¼-½ teaspoon salt

Bring 1 cup of water to a boil. While waiting for the water to boil, blend the rest of the ingredients (nuts, onion powder, cornstarch, nutritional yeast flakes, Bragg Liquid Aminos, and salt) until smooth in ½ cup of water. Add the blended mixture to a saucepan with the boiling water. Stir over low heat until thickened.

Per ¼-cup serving: 163 calories, 14.5g fat (3.4g saturated fat), 0mg cholesterol, 265mg sodium, 25.8g carbs, 1.9g dietary fiber, 0.3g sugar, 3.8g protein

ROASTED ALMOND BUTTER

ALMOND BUTTER IS ONE OF THE EASIEST THINGS TO MAKE IN THIS COOKBOOK. IT'S DECIDEDLY NOT THE EASIEST TO CLEAN UP, BUT WELL WORTH THE TROUBLE. ALMOND BUTTER IS (IN MY OPINION) MUCH TASTIER THAN PEANUT BUTTER, AND ALSO PROVIDES A HEFTY DOSE OF VITAMIN E. YOU MAY HAVE AVOIDED IT ON STORE SHELVES BECAUSE OF ITS HIGH PRICE TAG, BUT I HOPE THIS SIMPLE RECIPE WILL CONVINCE YOU TO GIVE IT A TRY. IF YOU PREFER THE FLAVOR OF RAW ALMONDS, YOU CAN SKIP AHEAD TO THE SECOND PARAGRAPH OF THE INSTRUCTIONS.

Makes 2 cups

4 cups raw almonds

¼ teaspoon salt

3 tablespoons agave nectar, optional

Preheat oven to 350°F. Evenly spread almonds in a single layer on a baking sheet and roast for 12 minutes. Immediately transfer the roasted almonds into a food processor and add the salt and agave nectar.

Blend until the mixture is smooth, occasionally stopping to wipe down the sides of the food processor. Don't worry if the mixture looks too dry or thick. The almonds will first turn into a powder, then a dough ball, and eventually into a smooth butter.

Pour into a glass container and lightly tap the base of the container on the countertop to bring the air bubbles to the surface. Store in the refrigerator for up to three months.

Per tablespoon: 74 calories, 5.9g fat (0.4g saturated fat), 0mg cholesterol, 20mg sodium, 4.1g carbs, 1.5g dietary fiber, 2g sugar, 2.5g protein

PART FIVE *the extras*

Acknowledgments

This book represents the efforts of a wonderful team of people whose big, ambitious hearts turned this dream of a book into a beautiful reality.

Warmest thanks to...

Editor: Sarah Jung

Design & Layout: Erin Engle

Contributing Writers: Sarah Jung, Jonathan Ewald, Ashley Kim, Midori Yoshimura, Danny Kwon, and Desiree McSherry

Medical Advisers: Randall Bivens, MD; Lorayne Barton, MD

Video production: Danny Kwon, Branden Albertson, Adam Oliver, and Rachel Ewald

Food styling and photography: Danny Kwon, Sung-Hoon Kang, Sarah Jung, Erin Engle, Joy Asumen-Carpenter, Branden Albertson, and Crystal Um

Project generously underwritten by: Naren James, MD; Todd Guthrie, MD; Donn Latour, MD; Brian Schwartz, MD; Lorayne Barton, MD; John Chung, MD and Randall Bivens, MD

Friends and relatives who were generous enough to share their favorite recipes and ideas: Neva Brackett, Sharon Cho, Rachelle Diaz, Ashley Kim, Danny Kwon, Kimberly Ewald, Erin Engle, Lena Williams, Darlene Niderost, Carmen Nashland, Cindy Magan, Sarah Jung, Lorayne Barton, MD; and Michelle Irwin

My dear family: Randy, Alec, Cristian, and Savannah

Index 5.2